Succulents at Home

THE COUNTRYMAN PRESS
A division of W. W. Norton & Company
Independent Publishers Since 1923

Succulents at Home

JOHN TULLOCK

Choosing, Growing, and
Decorating with the
Easiest Houseplants Ever

COUNTRY MAN KNOW HOW

For information about permission to reproduce selections from this book, write to
Permissions, The Countryman Press, 500 Fifth Avenue, New York, NY 10110

For information about special discounts for bulk purchases, please contact
W. W. Norton Special Sales at specialsales@wwnorton.com or 800-233-4830

Manufacturing by Versa Press
Series book design by Nick Caruso Design
Production manager: Devon Zahn

The Countryman Press
www.countrymanpress.com

A division of W. W. Norton & Company, Inc.
500 Fifth Avenue, New York, NY 10110
www.wwnorton.com

978-1-68268-384-2 (pbk.)

10 9 8 7 6 5 4 3 2 1

DEDICATION

This book is dedicated to gardeners everywhere, without whom
the world would be less beautiful.

CONTENTS

CHAPTER 1

Introduction

Trends in interior design come and go. I am fortunate to have been around when houseplants enjoyed a resurgence of their Gilded Age popularity in the 1970s, as well as today, when enhancing our indoor spaces with living plants is once again all the rage. As our world becomes increasingly urbanized and manufactured, we feel less and less connected to the natural world in our daily lives. "Bringing the outdoors in" by growing houseplants offers a great way to brighten a room, clear the air, relieve stress, and improve one's outlook.

The purpose of this book is to help anyone get started growing succulents indoors. While some succulent varieties can survive outdoors in the temperate zone, most are not frost hardy. I will therefore limit coverage to succulents that thrive as houseplants. The plants included here will benefit from spending the warmer months outside, if possible, but should be brought indoors again before the first frost.

Succulents: The "Perfect" Houseplants

Houseplant enthusiasts quickly learn that some groups of plants are better suited than others to indoor cultivation. Success with any plant—usually defined by its vigorous growth and periodic flowering—depends upon providing it with a reasonable facsimile of the conditions it would encounter in nature. For succulents, these conditions are easily met in the indoor environment. For some other types of plants, that is not the case. For example, low humidity indoors is often cited as a stress factor for tropical houseplants from rainforest habitats, such as some philodendrons and orchids. Succulents thrive in humidity levels that are most comfortable for humans, and even the warm, dry air from central heating suits them fine. Some houseplants require regular attention lest they suffer from drying out. Succulents are literally designed for drought tolerance. Succulents also do not need frequent repotting or fertilization in order to thrive. Most need repot-

ting only every few years, and feeding is necessary only a few times during the growing season. The vast majority of succulents thrive in arid conditions and thus can be maintained indoors in good condition with less bother than most other plant types. The ability to tolerate dry soil between infrequent periods of rainfall means that succulents growing in containers do not require daily attention to prevent them from drying out. And their adaptation to poor, mineralized soils means succulents can cope with low levels of fertilization that would cause many other plants to turn yellow and die.

Taken together with their intriguing forms, subtle color palette, and slow growth rate, their ease of culture makes succulents the best choice for an indoor gardener with a busy schedule. Succulents, therefore, might just be some of the most satisfactory houseplants available.

What Are Succulents?

Plants that have the ability to store water in their stems or leaves against periods of drought compose the arbitrary group known as "succulents." Just because two plants resemble each other in their water storage abilities does not mean they are necessarily related botanically. Because the traits shared by all these plants are the result of adaptations to arid environments, we find succulent members in several of the plant families recognized by botanists. For example, both cacti and euphorbias store water in their stems and both have spines, but they are only distant cousins botanically. Botanical distinctions are based largely upon the structure of flowers. Thus, the string of pearls plant, a popular succulent, reveals its affinity to other members of the aster family when it blooms. The flowers are structurally similar to other members of the family, such as dandelions. Flowers are adapted to facilitate pollination and thus the perpetuation of a given plant species. They do not function as water storage organs. Having leaves and/or stems capable of water storage is the trait that makes a plant a succulent, regardless of its floral anatomy.

Not all plants that store water should be considered succulents, either. For our purposes, I have limited the definition to plants that use their green leaves or stems for water storage. Many plants are capable of storing water in their fleshy roots or in underground stems called tubers, but we do not consider them to be succulents because the storage organs lie hidden beneath the soil. The technical name for this group of plants whose subterranean structures store water is "geophytes." However, some geophytes, which produce a structure known as a "caudex," can be considered succulents. The caudex is an above-ground storage organ derived from the stem, the root, or a combination of both. Because some of these plants, called "caudaciforms," are relatively common in the horticultural trade, I have included them here.

I should also note that plants can experience a lack of water amid its seeming abundance.

Some succulents are adapted for life in rainforest conditions, where they grow attached to trees or rocks with exposed roots that dry out rapidly after each rain. This group of succulents requires frequent watering but must not be allowed to sit in soggy soil. Several interesting members of the cactus family fall into this category and are discussed in a separate section explaining their peculiar growing requirements. Unlike desert cacti, these atypical cacti need frequent watering and feeding. Nevertheless, caring for them is easy and straightforward, and the reward is a spectacular bloom show. Thus, they have been popular houseplants for decades.

SUCCULENT PLANT FAMILIES

Unsurprisingly, the majority of succulents come from a limited number of plant families. This makes sense because the ability to develop the necessary adaptations for water storage is inherited. Plants lacking the various genes that confer these adaptations for water storage ability are at a disadvantage in an arid environment. Plants that are genetically capable, the "early adopters" of certain adaptations, as it were, come to dominate the flora in a given location. The species covered in this book belong to ten families, but the majority of species are in the stonecrop and cactus families, Crassulaceae and Cactaceae, respectively, with the remainder about evenly distributed among the other eight families.

Some succulent families are widespread, while others have an extremely limited range. For example, stonecrops (Crassulaceae) range from Africa and Europe east through Asia, and are also found in North America. On the other hand, 97 percent of species of ice plants (Aizoaceae) are found only in southern Africa. Plant collectors have brought a genuinely diverse array of succulent plants into the horticultural trade over the last couple of centuries, so that wild populations, thankfully, are no longer the source of plants in commerce. Overzealous collecting for the commercial trade has in some cases threatened the survival of wild succulent species. Wildlife officials recently seized a large number of succulent plants illegally harvested from the California coast. These plants were destined for collectors in China and Southeast Asia. Because some succulents grow very slowly, nursery-propagated plants may be scarce and expensive, creating a market for illegally harvested specimens. But not all succulents present this problem for growers. Indeed, many succulents are easy to propagate, as you will learn in Chapter 3, making them excellent candidates for large-scale production of plants for the horticulture trade. Certain species are sufficiently adaptable that they will grow—or at least survive—with indifferent care and downright neglect. As one might expect, these species have come to dominate the trade and are the varieties you are most likely to see when shopping your local garden center. Easy-care succulents also frequently turn up in displays at big-box retailers and supermarkets. Some, such as the Christmas cactus, have become holiday season staples. All of these commonly cultivated varieties are also great plants for beginners, being forgiving of an occasional mistake in cultivation.

If you are the type of person who prefers the out-of-the-ordinary, you can find an almost overwhelming abundance of succulents to purchase online. Many are no more difficult to grow than their more commonly seen counterparts but for various reasons have not attracted widespread interest. Some, on the other hand, can be extremely challenging, even for experts. To avoid disappointment, always carefully research the growth requirements for any plant you might be considering. In the plant catalog (see Chapter 5) I have noted special requirements, if any, for each of the varieties listed.

Following are descriptions of the ten families of succulents covered in this book. Most of the varieties not covered will also fall into one of these families. Some additional plant families have a few succulent members that may turn up from time to time.

Aizoaceae (EYE-zo-A-cee-ee): The ice plant family is largely native to southern Africa. From this group some of the most interesting succulents, known as "living stones," are widely available from well-stocked nurseries. These plants are not as forgiving as most succulents are and should be attempted after you have gained some experience. They are difficult to resist, as they manage to mimic smooth, water-worn pebbles almost perfectly.

Aloaceae (AL-oh-A-cee-ee): Aloes are native mostly to Africa and are widely cultivated as medicinal plants. The one you are most likely to encounter is *Aloe vera*, or "true aloe." The ability of this plant's juices to soothe minor burns and scrapes has been recognized for centuries. The leaves are borne in a rosette that in some species exceeds 6 feet in diameter. Most cultivated species are small enough for a 12-inch pot or smaller.

Apocynaceae (APP-OH-sine-a-cee-ee): The dogbane family includes many familiar plants, such as the native American milkweeds. Flowers among the succulent members of this group are among the most unusual ones you are likely to encounter. Although slow growing, most of the succulent dogbanes are undemanding houseplants. The ones of interest are from Africa, south Asia, and Australia. This group has undergone extensive taxonomic revision in recent years, and some names that may be familiar to experienced growers have changed. The names used here are most likely to be encountered in the nursery trade, which tends to lag a few years behind botanical research.

Asparagaceae (ass-PAR-a-GAY-cee-ee): The familiar spring vegetable, asparagus, has numerous botanical relatives. Among them are the agaves of the American Southwest and South America, and

Opposite page, clockwise from top left: Aizoaceae, Aloaceae, Apocynaceae, Asparagaceae

the African sansevierias. They are tough, durable plants and widely available.

Asphodelaceae (ASS-fo-dell-A-cee-ee): This group, which has no common name, is related to the previous one, Asparagaceae. The genera *Gasteria* and *Haworthia*, both from South Africa, are the most commonly available members. Haworthias are popular and rank among the most durable succulent houseplants you might choose.

Asteraceae (Ass-ter-A-cee-ee): Asters are found all over the world, and there are numerous species. For our purposes, three species of *Senecio*, all from South Africa, will be the most commonly encountered succulent ones. None presents any special challenge to the grower.

Cactaceae (Kak-TAY-cee-ee): Cacti are distributed almost exclusively in the New World. Of the 1,700–plus species, only one, *Rhipsalis baccifera*, is found in both Africa and Sri Lanka. All cacti possess specially modified branches, or "aureoles," from which both spines and flowers arise. Not all cacti live in arid habitats. The *Schlumbergera* genus, for example, lives in rainforests and gives us the popular "holiday" cacti, sold in bloom from Thanksgiving through Christmas. Cactus flowers range from insignificant to spectacular and are usually the primary object of cultivating them. But whether in bloom or not, cacti will endear you with their interesting forms and their tenacity as container subjects.

Crassulaceae (Krass-ooh-LAY-cee-ee): Stonecrops sometimes literally live on stones, but they can be found in many locations where thin, rapidly draining soils are predominant. They are found either in the Northern Hemisphere or in South Africa, with multiple species in both temperate and tropical regions. Because so many members of this family are cultivated as houseplants, I have reserved additional discussion of them to the plant catalog section (see Chapter 5). For now, it is sufficient to say you are unlikely to enter the world of succulent gardening without encountering this group. Crassulas, as they are collectively known, even have their own special physiological adaptations to growth in arid climates. Crassulacean acid metabolism, or CAM photosynthesis, was discovered in and named for this group. In brief, the adaptation allows plants to keep their stomata (leaf pores) closed during the daytime in order to avoid water loss. At night, the plants open their stomata, admitting air. They are able to store atmospheric carbon dioxide in the form of a four-carbon compound, malate. The malate is held within special intracellular compartments called "vacuoles." During the day, the malate is transported to the cell's chloroplasts, where the stored carbon dioxide is then enzymatically released from the malate and

Opposite page, clockwise from top left: Asphodelaceae, Asteraceae, Cactaceae, Crassulaceae

HYBRIDIZATION

Horticulturists frequently create artificial hybrids by crossing two closely related plant species in the hope of obtaining offspring with the desirable characteristics of both. As a general rule, hybridization can only occur between members of the same botanical family. Pollen from one species is transferred to the female flower parts of another species in the hope of producing viable seed. The offspring grown from such seeds will be hybrids of the two parent species. Some may not survive to maturity. Some may look much like one parent or the other. If the hybridizer is lucky, a few seedlings will have the desired combination of characteristics. These will be selected for further propagation and/or breeding. Owing to their wide popularity, succulents have been the subjects of numerous hybridizations by horticulturists seeking new and interesting forms. You can identify hybrids by their naming convention: ×*Echeveria* refers to a cross between two species of *Echeveria*, for example. Hybrids may also be created between different genera of succulents within the same family. Thus ×*Gastroveria* is a cross between *Gastropetalum* and *Echeveria*. Note that some growers omit the × in front of the name. You may see *Gastrosedum*, for example. Hybrids typically offer distinct colors or leaf shapes, and may be more vigorous and easier to grow than their respective parents. Those with superior horticultural merit are given a cultivar name. ("Cultivar" is a contraction of "cultivated variety.") These named cultivars are worth seeking out for your collection. Cultivar names are enclosed in single quotation marks. Thus, one popular hybrid cultivar is ×*Gastroveria* 'Debbie.' It forms rosettes of flattened leaves with pointed tips and a lovely pinkish-purple pigmentation.

Left: Euphorbiaceae; right: Orchids

utilized for photosynthesis. CAM photosynthesis has been identified in some other succulent plant families and in a few nonsucculent plants.

Euphorbiaceae (You-FOR-bee-A-cee-ee): Spurges, as the members of this family are known, are dis-tributed worldwide. Perhaps the most familiar example will be the poinsettia, sold by the millions for Christmas decoration. The most popular house-plants from this family come from South Africa. Spurges lack the aureoles that are characteristic of cacti. Like cacti, though, spurges often have spines,

and they also exude a white, sticky sap that can be irritating to some people. The members of this family that are included in the plant catalog (Chapter 5) are undemanding houseplants, and some of them can achieve an impressively large size, even under somewhat adverse conditions.

Orchids: No book about succulents would be complete without mention of orchids. Although they are seldom found in arid climates, orchids share many of the adaptations that we find in other succulents, namely water-storage organs derived from the stem. Tropical orchids typically live perched on the limbs of trees, where their roots dry out quickly after a rain. Many have evolved special water-storage organs, known as "pseudobulbs," and thus can be classified as succulents. While I will make reference to a few orchids that can grow alongside other succulents on your windowsill, the cultivation of orchids as a group is a suitable topic for another complete book. Indeed, many hundreds of books about orchids and their horticulture exist. If you get hooked on the orchid family, there is no shortage of information and advice for growing them in your home.

SUCCULENT FORMS AND COLORS

For beginners, I recommend succulents that lack spines. They are easy to handle but may or may not have showy flowers. Spiny succulents, ironically, often produce the largest, showiest blooms. Non-spiny succulents engage our attention and appreciation through their sculptural forms and intriguing coloration rather than their floral display.

The most obvious feature of non-spiny succulents is their smooth, fleshy leaves. They can appear to be made of wax and come in a range of colors. Every shade of green, from deep, rich pine to fluorescent warning paint, occurs in some member of this group. Plus, the range of colors extends to reds, purples, steely blues, and shocking pink. Horticulturists have succeeded in producing a sufficient range of hybrids and selections that you are likely to fill all the available space in your home without including an example of every one of them.

Broadly categorized, the nongreen pigments found in the leaves of succulents serve to protect them from too much damaging ultraviolet or infrared radiation. Red pigments, for example, help to reflect heat (infrared) away from the leaf surface. Thick white coatings of waxy scales or a fine powder may cover some plants. This too is a form of "sunscreen." The leaves of succulents may be enclosed in a tough, waxy skin that helps to reduce moisture loss and gives the plant the appearance of polished leather. Compared to more typical plants, succulents have leaves with fewer breathing pores, or "stomata." This helps conserve water, which escapes via these pores when the plant exchanges gases with the atmosphere.

Opposite page: Cattleya orchids grow on tree limbs in a tropical rainforest

The shapes of succulent leaves and stems, apart from their obvious fleshiness, may derive from a variety of adaptations in addition to water conservation. Among the most remarkable are those that give the plant the appearance of a stone, which is thought to provide protection from predation as the plants grow among pebbles, often in dry creek beds. The smooth, rounded shapes of the leaves of many species may also provide this form of camouflage, as leaf-munching herbivores apparently do not recognize them as food despite an upright growth habit. Color patterns that seem almost reptilian may serve a similar function. Spines, noxious sap, and the irritating little hairs called glochidia produced by some cacti are all adaptations for deterring predators. In the arid environments where most succulents live, the plants are living reservoirs of water and nutrients that would soon succumb to predation without these safeguards.

SUCCULENTS IN HORTICULTURE

Like that of all flowering plants, the life of a succulent begins with a seed. When the seed encounters favorable conditions, it germinates, and if all goes well it grows into a plant that will one day produce seeds of its own, completing the life cycle. Because they are popular horticulture subjects, however, many succulents have life cycles that can diverge significantly from the natural pattern, thanks to human caretakers.

In an ever-expanding quest for new and interesting forms to entice customers, horticulturists can rely on two methods: selection and hybridization. Selection involves growing a large number of seeds to maturity and culling the resulting plants for desirable traits. The process is analogous to the process of evolution that has resulted in the array of plants that we have on earth today, more than a million species. Each new generation expresses new combinations of genes. Most of the time plants breed true to type, but frequently there are subtle variations that may be of interest to the horticulturist. Perhaps one plant is strikingly different from its siblings. It may be on the way to fame and stardom as a horticultural variety, assuming it can pass muster under additional criteria, such as being undemanding in its cultivation requirements.

When an individual seedling achieves this kind of horticultural distinction as a "selection," it may be given a name by the breeder or someone else interested in distinguishing the plant in the marketplace. Thus, *Echeveria subrigida* 'Red Tide' is a selection of the species with red edging and twisted leaves.

The other method of creating new types of succulents is hybridization, discussed previously. Crossing two species or genera adds a large amount of variability to the genetics of the offspring, increasing the likelihood of unique or interesting new forms. Because the horticulturist has control over the process, hybridization may be undertaken with a specific goal in mind, such as increasing the hardiness of a particular line of plants or introducing a new color into the floral palette of a given species.

The possibilities are endless, and the vast selection of hybrid plants available to consumers is a testament to the effectiveness of the technique.

Once the grower has obtained a plant having the desired suite of characteristics, it will be propagated for commercial sale by one of a variety of vegetative propagation techniques. This results in the production of identical clones of the original plant, all preserving the same desirable characteristics. The best quality succulents for your money are likely to be these cloned offspring of named cultivars. The advantage of naming cultivars is that growers all over the world can compare notes, knowing they are talking about the same genetic line of plants. While grocery and big-box retail stores may carry the most common and popular cultivars, they rarely label them as such. Your best bet for finding good specimens of named varieties is a nursery or garden center that caters to a more experienced clientele.

Hobby gardeners can use the same techniques of vegetative propagation to increase the number of plants in their collection, as discussed in Chapter 3.

What Makes Succulents So Great?

Succulents offer so much to the houseplant enthusiast that their popularity is unsurprising. Their special adaptations serve them well in the modern

indoor environment. Contrary to popular belief, many succulents do not require extreme sunshine in order to thrive and so can be used in locations other than a south-facing window. Some smaller succulent plants actually grow in the shade of larger plants in their natural habitat, and thus will grow indoors in an east or west window. Because of their adaptations to unforgiving environments, succulents can get by for long periods with very little water and no fertilizer, simply by not growing. This means you have a considerable amount of control over the size of the plants in your collection. You can keep them small by withholding fertilizer and leaving them in a cramped pot, or you can repot and feed them regularly and watch them grow into large specimens. For many succulent varieties, the choice of how fast they grow is up to you.

Perhaps most appealingly, succulents look great with a wide variety of home decor finishes, fabrics, and surfaces. They are equally at home in a modern minimalist design or a more traditional one. They can be grown in old shoes, discarded food containers, crates, pallets, in frames on the wall, and in wreaths on the front door. They do well in hanging baskets, sconce pots, and tiny terrariums, or in big, roomy containers of any design or material.

It requires little skill or practice to succeed with succulents. All you need is the willingness to follow a few simple steps to success, customizing your succulent collection to align with your space and circumstances. I recently read about a collection of nearly 100 succulents that live in a 300-square-foot motor home with their human family. Even a tiny apartment should be able to accommodate a small collection. Last spring, every supermarket and big-box retailer in my neighborhood had a display of potted succulents out front. Succulents are turning up everywhere, and they are proving hard to resist. Are you also tempted to give them a try?

Give in to the temptation and join in the fun of growing hardy, beautiful succulents.

CHAPTER 2

Growing Succulents

Succulents are ideal houseplants because their needs are simple. In this chapter, I will discuss what those needs are and how to provide them so your plants will not only survive but thrive.

What Succulents Need

The chief requirement for successfully growing succulents indoors is providing them with a sufficiency of water, but not too much. Succulents are drought tolerant but do not tolerate a soggy root space. Beyond that, if you have a sunny spot, such as a south-facing window, you should be able to grow most of the plants mentioned in this book. In addition, several members of the succulent clan will thrive in partial shade year-round. These species may actually be damaged by too much sun and are good candidates for growing in an east- or west-facing window.

If you are able to give them a sojourn outdoors during warm weather, many succulents, especially cacti, can be successfully carried through the winter months with minimal sunshine. Even a north-facing window will do while the plants are in their dormant, resting phase during the winter months. Sometimes, the transition from a cool, cloudy winter to a warm, sunny spring will induce your plant to bloom. Cactus flowers are frequently showy and often are larger than one might expect from the size of the plant. Thus, some gardeners find them irresistible.

All succulents will benefit from outdoor living if that is an option for you. A balcony, patio, deck, or porch will suit them just fine. Even a window box will provide more sun and fresh air than the plants would get sitting indoors in front of the same window. Just be sure, when moving any plant from indoors to out, to expose them to sun gradually, or you risk damaging the foliage from sunburn. I like to begin with only two hours of exposure in the

The center of this Brassavola *leaf has been scorched by too much sun*

morning, moving the plants to a shady location for the remainder of the day. After a week, assuming no ill effects, I increase the exposure to four hours per day. After a week of that, the plants are usually ready for a full day of sun. Solar intensity varies greatly with latitude and the time of year. I move my plants outdoors about a month after the vernal equinox, and I live in Tennessee. If you live farther south or move plants outdoors later in the season, you may want to take more precautions to prevent sunburn.

Succulents outdoors are exposed to different hazards than those they might face indoors. Harsh weather can do physical damage, overturning pots and snapping tender branches. Stray animals may also cause problems. It may come as a surprise, but the greatest danger your plants face outdoors is getting too much water from frequent rains. If you live in an area that receives abundant rainfall,

consider keeping your plants under a shelter of some kind so you can remain in control of their watering schedule. In my case, an inch a week is about average in summer, and I am careful to bring plants indoors to dry off for a few days if I think they are staying too moist.

Choosing Containers

Anything that resists moisture and is of sufficient capacity can be pressed into service as a plant container. Succulents come in all sizes, and you will need containers of various size if you intend to assemble a collection. The first consideration in selecting a container is to choose a size suitable for the root ball of the plant you wish to accommodate. Do not go overboard, however, as a too-large container may hold too much moisture around the plant's roots, a condition that can spell disaster for most species. As a rule of thumb, choose a container with a diameter about half the height of the plant. Thus, a jade plant (*Crassula ovata*) 16 inches in height should fit nicely in an 8-inch pot. Another good rule when repotting is to choose a pot 2 inches in diameter larger than the previous one. This allows for an inch of fresh soil all the way around the root ball.

The pot's proportions should also be given consideration. From an aesthetic viewpoint, a tall, narrow container is better suited to displaying a tall, columnar plant, whereas a short, squat container looks better with a similarly compact inhabitant. Interesting effects can also be achieved when this rule is ignored, however. Therefore, feel free to use whatever suits your fancy and seems reasonable for the plant you have. While certain succulents undoubtedly do better with room in the pot for deeper roots, most of them can manage just fine with whatever amount of space is available, provided they are receiving adequate care. Images of succulents growing in their natural habitat frequently depict them clinging to life in a shallow depression among rocks or in an otherwise restricted space, eking out an existence with only a small amount of soil.

For maximum visual appeal, the material and color of the container you choose should reflect either the colors of the plant itself or the overall decor of the indoor space in which you expect to display the plant. For example, for the same plant you might choose a container in a strongly contrasting color to make a bold statement, or a neutral color to allow the plant to take center stage, or a harmonious shade of the same hue as the plant to create a mood. A rustic wooden crate filled with a variety of succulents might look better if painted to match the woodwork in the room. In a different setting, the crate might look better left unfinished. That is the beauty of working with succulents in interior design. Because of their unique ability to withstand harsh conditions, succulents can be displayed in ways that would kill many other houseplants. For example, succulents

can be used to create a living wreath for a door or table decoration (see page 80 for instructions). Succulent "pictures" can be created within frames that surround a shallow layer of growing medium (page 86). Succulents are often the main plants in vertical gardens displayed on walls or fences, again owing to their ability to grow with a minimum of soil and water. The possibilities are limited only by your imagination.

Growing Media

Succulents can be grown in a wide range of media, from pure sand to commercial potting mix. They will thrive best with a well-drained medium that does not hold too much moisture. For the beginning gardener, select a commercial mix that is intended for succulents. Often, such a mix will be labeled for use with palms, cacti, and avocados. One major commercial brand with which I have had good results comprises 50 percent timber processing waste (bark and wood chips), 25 percent peat moss, 15 percent sand, and 10 percent perlite. I have also had success with combinations of nonorganic materials, particularly fine gravel, calcined clay, and sand, in roughly equal proportions. This mixture is preferred for more fussy plants that are especially sensitive to overwatering. The inert mix is also great for a terrarium, as it does not break down and hold moisture, a problem with mixes that contain a high proportion of organic matter. Because a terrarium can lose water only via

evaporation, materials that do not retain water are preferred. Plant-derived potting mixes are also more attractive to fungus gnats, which don't harm plants but nevertheless are undesirable for a terrarium or indeed any houseplant collection. Nevertheless, if you are just beginning with a succulent collection, I recommend sticking with the commercial mix until you gain experience.

Avoid using garden soil if at all possible. Adding soil to a container mix brings in weed seeds and potential plant pests, and thus causes more problems than are solved by the small amount of plant nutrients it supplies. If you must use soil, sterilize it by placing it in a disposable aluminum turkey roaster and heating it in the oven at 325°F for an hour.

For succulent projects with a short life span, such as wreaths or table decorations, long fiber sphagnum moss or coconut fiber (coir) are suitable growing media, either in addition to potting mix or as the sole substrate for the roots. The purpose of including these fibrous materials is to anchor the roots of the plants and to retain moisture while allowing plenty of air to reach roots. Arrangements in such media will need more frequent watering than those in potting mix. Since neither the moss nor the coir provide much in the way of plant nutrients, it will also be necessary to feed more frequently than would otherwise be the case. On the other hand, it may be desirable to limit the growth of such displays after they have filled their containers. This can be accomplished by limiting fertilizer additions to once every two or three months. Growing plants in reduced light, so long as they don't show signs of distress, will also slow their growth.

Perhaps the most important thing to remember about growing media is that each one will require a different strategy when watering plants. Different media dry out at different rates. Therefore, it makes sense to settle upon one growing medium for all the plants in your collection, at least until you have gained experience in determining when to water your plants for maximum health and growth.

The water retention properties of the growing medium will determine how quickly it dries out after watering. As a general rule, the larger the proportion of organic matter in the mix, the slower it will dry out. I suggest not exceeding one-half of the total volume in organic matter under any circumstances. Less may be better, depending upon the sensitivity of your plant selection to soil moisture. If your living space has higher than normal humidity, you may want a fast-drying mix for the plants.

A good general-purpose mix is equal parts fine pine bark chips, calcined clay, and perlite. To increase drainage properties even more, substitute fine gravel for some of the bark chips.

Whether you mix your own growing medium or rely on bagged commercial products, the best approach is to select one and stick with it. That way, you will learn its water retention properties and can keep your plants at their optimum moisture level.

MEDIUM PLUS CONTAINER

You can control how often you need to water your succulent collection by choosing the right combination of growing medium and container. If the growing medium retains water, that is, it has a high proportion of organic matter, choose containers made of porous materials or that are designed to facilitate drainage. The classic would be unglazed terra cotta, but wood, wire baskets, and orchid pots with extra openings will all encourage the growing medium to dry out rapidly. On the other hand, if you are using a fast-draining potting medium made mostly of inert ingredients, choose containers that help retain moisture, such as those composed of plastic, glazed porcelain, or metal. Otherwise, you may find your plant requires frequent watering. Regardless of container type, it should have drainage holes in the bottom to prevent plant roots from standing in water.

PROTECTING YOUR FURNITURE

Any houseplant in a container can damage your furniture with leaked water or soil stains. Use plastic or ceramic saucers underneath plants to catch any drips, or set plants in cachepots with a layer of gravel or Styrofoam pieces in the bottom to keep the plant's roots from touching standing water. Rinse out the gravel or foam periodically and allow it to dry out thoroughly before replacing it to eliminate stagnation, which leads to algae or mold growth.

CONTAINERS LACKING DRAINAGE

With care, it is possible to grow succulents in containers without any drainage holes. Watering at the proper rate is crucial in this case. Start with a well-watered plant, and then check each week for soil moisture. You can do this in several ways. You can purchase a moisture meter at a garden center or online. This device features a probe you stick into the soil, and the meter tells you how much water is present. You can also poke your finger into the growing medium, although this can be too disruptive for a small arrangement. Another method is to use a piece of absorbent wood. A popsicle stick or a paint-stir stick work well. Insert the wood into the growing medium and withdraw it after a few moments. You can then easily tell if the soil contains moisture from the appearance of the wood.

REPOTTING

If you bring a plant home from the garden center, unless you intend to repot it immediately you will be stuck with whatever medium and container was used by the store. Likely, the container will be plastic and the medium will be one based on peat moss and perlite. These tend to hold moisture and make the nursery's job of maintaining plants easier—the less often they need to be watered, the less labor required to produce them. When the plants arrive on your windowsill, they will be subjected to different conditions of light, humidity, and air circulation than they were previously, and this, too, will affect the rate at which they utilize moisture.

Eventually, your plants will need repotting, or you may want to put your plant into something more decorative than the plastic nursery pot right away. Doing so affords you the opportunity to choose a combination of potting medium and container that works best with the watering schedule you find most convenient. Here, the rule is to choose an impervious container to go with a more sharply drained growing medium, or a porous container with a medium that is more moisture retentive. For example, if you choose a commercial potting medium that contains peat moss—one national brand is about 50 percent—it is probably wise to use plain terra cotta pots, as their porosity allows them to dry more quickly. On the other hand, if you want a glazed ceramic pot, select a growing medium with ingredients that promote drainage. These include sand, gravel, perlite, and calcined clay products.

Whenever you repot, choose a container that is only slightly larger than the old one, or the growing medium may remain too moist while roots are in the process of growing into it. Succulents grow slowly, as a rule, and it can take more than one season for the roots to fill the pot. As a general rule, plan to repot mature plants every three years. Younger plants grow faster than mature ones and should be repotted annually.

COMPONENTS OF GROWING MEDIA

Sand: Coarse builder's sand or children's play sand are both available in 40-pound bags. Sand can be added to peat-based growing media to improve drainage. It also adds weight, a consideration if containers are located outdoors for a portion of the year. A heavy container is less likely to tip in high wind. On the other hand, a container that is too heavy will be difficult to relocate when the weather turns cold. A cubic foot of sand weighs about 100 pounds. Sand also has a tendency to sink to the bottom of the container. Avoid using beach sand, as it is too fine and tends to compact. It also contains salt, gypsum, and possibly other components that your plants won't like. Although some succulents will grow in pure sand, as a rule sand should be used as a decorative element in succulent containers, rather than as a component of the growing medium.

Gravel: The term "gravel" can cover a lot of territory, from coarse sand to chunks the size of a dime. For potting mix, gravel with an average diameter of $\frac{1}{16}$ to $\frac{1}{8}$ inch is best. You can purchase gravel of various sizes in bags at both well-stocked garden centers and aquarium shops. The latter often have a wide selection of natural gravel that can be used both as a component of potting media and as a mulch. Adding fine gravel to the growing medium will improve drainage. Particles added to the growing medium should average about $\frac{1}{16}$ inch in diameter for best results. Do not use fine gravel as a surface mulch, as it inhibits evaporation too much. Instead, use pebbles from about ¼ inch to 1 inch in diameter. Gravel does not separate out from the rest of the medium as readily as sand does.

Clockwise from top left: sand, gravel, calcined clay, bark; center: perlite

Perlite: Perlite is a volcanic glass that has been subjected to heat treatment, causing it to expand into something resembling pellets of Styrofoam. It is a common component of commercial potting mixes, as it is lightweight and promotes good drainage. Although completely inert and effective in improving drainage, perlite has the annoying property of buoyancy. Some growers avoid it, as it has the habit of floating to the surface and spoiling the appearance. The best way to deal with this issue is to mulch the surface of the pot with sand, gravel, stones, or a combination of those. Despite its drawbacks, perlite has become ubiquitous, and you will probably find it in any commercial potting medium you select. You can use perlite to modify standard houseplant potting mix, the kind you might find in the grocery store, for use with succulents. Simply add one part perlite to three parts potting mix.

Calcined clay products: Calcined clay products are natural clay minerals that have been subjected to heat. This process creates a porous material that is milled into various sizes and resembles gravel. However, unlike gravel, calcined clays are absorbent. Adding this material to potting mix increases its moisture retentiveness, although not to the extent that an organic material does. Another characteristic of calcined clay is its ability to bind important minerals, making them available to plant roots each time the plant is watered. These products have been utilized in horticulture in Asia for years and have only recently begun to attract the attention of American plant enthusiasts. Calcined clay is commonplace here, though: Many brands of cat litter are based on it. If you choose to use it in this form, avoid the scented or clumping types and select a basic, no-frills product.

Organic matter: Among the various organic materials that can be included in growing media for succulents, the most common ones are peat moss and products derived from lumber processing. They are added to media for the purpose of increasing water retention. Using them with succulents helps to extend the time between waterings, a benefit for anyone with a busy schedule. Like calcined clays, these materials also retain minerals, making them available to plant roots.

Peat moss is harvested from peat bogs, ancient accumulations of partially decomposed mosses that are often several feet deep. As a horticultural medium, peat moss has been around for a very long time, but in recent years questions have arisen as to the sustainability of harvesting mass quantities of it for the horticulture industry. Suppliers claim the rate of new peat formation is sufficient to replace what they take, but not everyone agrees. If this issue is of concern, just bear in mind that virtually all commercial horticultural media contain at least some peat. Coir fiber, which comes from coconut processing, is a substitute, though not completely satisfactory, as it does not absorb moisture as readily.

Lumber production creates great quantities of

by-products, most notably bark, along with sawdust. The latter is seldom used in horticultural products, as it breaks down quickly and can alter the pH of the mix dramatically. Bark chips, especially the smallest pieces, known as "fines," are a valuable component of many growing media. Partially composted pine bark fines are sold in 40-pound bags at many garden centers and big-box stores, and can be used to create your own growing medium from scratch. This material is also a major component of some commercially produced growing media for cacti and succulents.

Fertilizers

Succulents will respond to appropriate fertilization with growth and possibly flowering. Over-fertilization will lead to problems, such as yellowed foliage and damaged roots. However, if not fertilized, plants respond to a shortage of nutrients simply by refusing to grow. As long as they receive enough light and water, some succulents can go without food or growth for years. Therefore, always err on the side of too little when feeding your succulents. Most people will want to feed their plants in order to provoke growth or to prepare them for blooming. To accomplish this you have multiple options.

Many gardeners will choose organic fertilizers over the chemical ones. This is fine, as long as the plants receive appropriate nutrition. Over many years of gardening I have learned that plants do not distinguish between the sources of their nutrition, and a given amount of nitrogen applied as cottonseed meal will produce the same result as the same amount applied as ammonium nitrate. In terms of cost, chemical fertilizer wins hands down over organic. Choose the product you think is right for your situation.

It is easy to compare different fertilizers in terms of their cost. All you have to do is calculate the cost per unit of nitrogen supplied by the fertilizer. The math is not complicated, and all the information you require is printed on the product label. By law, fertilizers must be prominently labeled with their "NPK" numbers. This set of numbers reveals the percentage by weight of nitrogen (N), phosphorus (P), and potassium (K) supplied by the fertilizer. Granular "all-purpose" fertilizer is often a 10-10-10 formula. This translates to 10 percent nitrogen by weight, so a pound of the fertilizer contains 0.1 pound, or a bit less than 2 ounces, of nitrogen. If a 5-pound bag of this product costs $5—that is, $1 per pound—then the nitrogen costs $10 a pound, since you would need 10 pounds of the fertilizer to supply a pound of nitrogen. Similarly, if the fertilizer is low in nitrogen, say 1 percent, as is the case with earthworm castings, the cost of the nitrogen is considerably more. For example, if a 5-pound bag of worm castings costs $5, then 1 pound costs $1 and contains 0.01 pound of nitrogen. You would thus need 100 bags, or $500 worth, to obtain 1 pound of nitrogen from this product. It is not necessary to consider separately the costs of the phosphorus and potassium. Nitrogen is by far the most expensive component of any fertilizer, whether organic or not.

The best all-round choice for succulents being grown as houseplants is a balanced, soluble fertilizer. "Balanced" simply means the formula contains roughly equal quantities of nitrogen, phosphorus, and potassium. Thus, the 10-10-10 product just mentioned would be an example of a balanced formula. One major brand, Miracle-Gro, dominates the soluble fertilizer market, but you may find similar products under different brand names. If you prefer an organic fertilizer, look for granular formulations with at least 6 percent nitrogen.

Regardless of which food source you select for your succulents, you will not need much. Unless the goal is to force rapid growth, feeding is only required a few times during the growing season in the case of most succulents. Succulents that grow during summertime in the Northern Hemisphere should be fertilized as the weather begins to warm up in spring. Gardeners who move plants outdoors for the season should feed plants as soon as they are acclimated to bright sunshine. Additional feedings about once a month thereafter will suffice for the plant's needs throughout the season. As the weather cools and days shorten in autumn, the plants will enter winter dormancy. During this period, withhold all fertilizer, as the plant is not growing and does not need feeding. Also reduce watering. Be sure the soil is completely dry between waterings. Overly moist soil during the dormant period almost always leads to root rot.

Plants that originate in the Southern Hemisphere typically remain dormant in summer heat and make most of their growth during the winter months when cultivated in the north. They thus require feeding during winter. For these plants, a light feeding about once every six weeks should produce good growth. Some summer dormant species have been so long in cultivation they have adapted to the opposite schedule. As a rule, treat all plants you obtain from a garden center or nursery as summer growing unless the grower advises otherwise.

It is always a mistake to apply fertilizer when the plant is not actively growing. Not only are you wasting the fertilizer, but you may cause damage to the roots. When in doubt, do not feed. When you see new foliage bursting out, get out the fertilizer, but avoid the temptation to feed frequently.

You will gain nothing by exceeding the manufacturer's recommendations for dosing any fertilizer. In fact, label directions typically call for you to use more fertilizer than is strictly necessary. Perhaps this is a way of encouraging repeat sales. You can safely cut the recommended amount in half and still get good results with your plants. A few succulent varieties that live in extreme habitats, such as *Lithops* and *Fenestraria*, need only one-quarter of the recommended dosage. For example, soluble fertilizers are often formulated so that the recommended dosage is 1 teaspoon of the product per gallon of water. For most succulents, this can be cut to one-half teaspoon per gallon, and for the really slow-growing varieties, one-fourth teaspoon per gallon is sufficient. These dosages assume plants are fed every month to six weeks during the growing season.

If you prefer, use a timed-release fertilizer mixed into the potting medium. These products are made by enclosing plant nutrients in a clay shell, forming little spheres called prills. For an 8-inch pot, you only need about a half teaspoon of fertilizer prills every three or four months. Timed-release fertilizers will feed your plants for the entire growing season from a single dose. If you go this route, it is important to repot just as growth begins for maximal benefit from the fertilizer in the fresh potting mix. Carefully follow the manufacturer's instructions regarding the amount to use. Generally, the label provides a table indicating amounts for various pot sizes or volumes of growing medium. For these products, nutrients "leak" from the prills as they are taken up by the plant.

Pay attention to how plants respond to the fertilizer you choose, keeping notes as to the timing and amount of feeding, and soon you will develop a strategy that maximizes the health of your succulent collection without wasteful overfeeding.

Potting Succulents

Whether you are just bringing a new plant home from the store or have decided it is time to display one plant or a whole collection in new containers, the procedure for repotting is the same.

The best time to repot succulents is near the end of the plant's dormant period. For cacti and many other species, this will be during late winter or early spring. For winter-growing species, spring transplanting is usually successful, but the best time would be late autumn. The idea is always to disturb the plant's roots at a time when it is not making active growth, but when new growth will soon take place.

When moving a plant to a larger container, a procedure known as "potting up," select a container that is about 2 inches in diameter larger than the old pot. This will guarantee sufficient room for the roots to expand their territory. Avoid using a pot more than 2 inches larger than the old one, as this can lead to excess soil moisture and root rot.

If you are moving multiple plants to the same container to create an arrangement, try to maintain an inch "border" all around the edge of the pot to permit root development. Also leave a half inch or so between each individual root ball. Plants in containers always look better if they have room to "grow in" after you plant them.

To remove the plant from its old pot, support it near the soil level with your nondominant hand,

and with your dominant hand invert the pot so you basically have the top of the root ball in the palm of your nondominant hand. Rap the bottom of the pot sharply with the heel of your free hand or a handy object, and the plant should pop right out, roots and all. If it seems reluctant, run a kitchen knife blade around the perimeter of the pot to separate the root ball from the inner surface, then invert the pot as described and give it a whack. Stuck plants can be a problem with unglazed terra cotta or with wood containers, both of which have porous surfaces that offer purchase to the roots. If loosening the roots with a knife does not work, as a last resort break the pot if it is terra cotta, or cut the plant free if the pot is wood.

Have the new pot ready. I like to place a piece of plastic window screen over the drain hole to prevent the medium from washing out and to inhibit insects and other invertebrates that might seek shelter in the pot. Place a small amount of growing medium in the bottom of the pot, enough so that when pressed down firmly, it will support the plant's root ball at the correct height. The original soil line should be about a half inch to an inch lower than the rim of the new pot. This will allow for a little fresh potting mix on top and a layer of pebbles or other decorative materials.

Set the root ball into the new pot, centering the plant's top growth attractively, and support the plant with one hand as you add potting mix to the space between the root ball and the pot. Firm the mix with your fingers, filling the pot all the way up to the level of the old soil line, or just a tiny bit more. Finish off the surface with a mulch of sand, pebbles, or larger stones. Do not cover the entire soil surface too deeply, however, or the medium may remain too moist.

If you are repotting a plant with spines, you may find it helpful to have a blunt instrument to tamp the potting mix into the pot around the plant. Doing so allows you to keep your fingers far away from the spines.

If the plant was in the pot too long before transplanting, chances are the roots will have grown in a circle around the bottom of the root ball. To permit the roots to expand normally, loosen up the circling roots and spread them out in a more natural arrangement. It won't hurt to trim off a few of the roots if this will allow the whole mass to fit better into the new pot.

Once the plant is in its new container, water it well and set it in a shaded location for a few days. This will help it overcome the stress of having its roots disturbed. After a couple of days in shade, gradually expose the plant to more and more sunshine. You should be rewarded with the appearance of new growth within a month.

Step-by-Step: Potting Succulents

1. Support the plant by holding it at soil level with your nondominant hand.

2. Invert the pot so the surface of the root ball is in your nondominant hand.

3. With the heel of your other hand, sharply rap on the bottom of the pot. This should knock the plant free.

4. If the plant is stuck, run a knife blade around the perimeter of the pot to free it. Don't worry about a little root damage.

5. Place growing medium in the new pot and set the root ball on top of it. The old soil line should be about half an inch below the rim of the pot.

6. Support the plant with one hand while adding growing medium to the pot with the other. Press down gently but firmly and fill to the old soil line.

7. Add a final layer of growing medium or a mulch of pebbles or coarse sand.

8. Water the pot thoroughly and place the plant in indirect light to recover.

9. After a week, move the plant to your preferred location.

DEALING WITH DASTARDLY SPINES

A large number of succulents, including most cacti and euphorbias, have spines. These can range from soft and harmless to viciously sharp, barbed, and venomous. Given that the purpose of such spines is typically to fend off animals that might be tempted to eat the plants, it is not surprising that they will also fend off us humans. Although seldom serious enough to require medical attention, a jab from certain plants' spines can be exquisitely painful, and some cacti also produce very small spines designed to work themselves into the skin, producing maximal irritation.

Therefore, it is wise to always wear gloves when working with spiny succulents. Leather garden gloves are your best bet for most specimens. If you will be working with unusually large plants or plants with especially nasty spines, it is probably wise to purchase a pair of welder's gloves, which are impervious to anything the plants can muster.

Another approach is to handle plants with a pair of kitchen tongs. You may or may not find this convenient, depending upon your level of dexterity. Even if you hold the plant with tongs, you run the risk of poking your free hand when you try to add potting mix to the pot. I suggest always erring on the side of caution. Use a blunt piece of wood—a sawed-off handle from an old broom is ideal—to tamp the potting mix into the pot.

For small to medium specimens, you can also fold several thicknesses of newspaper into a "belt" that you can wrap around the plant to provide a spine-free place to hold it.

Another tip for transplanting spiny succulents is to use a stand-in until you have the soil in the new pot. Take an empty pot the same size as the old pot the plant is in. Add some growing mix to the bottom of the new pot and place the empty pot on it. Fill in around the empty pot, firming the soil with your fingers. Then remove the empty pot. Now you will have a cavity in the fresh growing mix that is exactly the size of the root ball you are transplanting. This permits a quick transfer from the old pot to the new, with minimal risk of contacting the spines. Nevertheless, wear some gloves.

Troubleshooting

Gardeners familiar with the more pest-prone members of the plant kingdom will rejoice to learn that succulents are seldom bothered by pests. Further, the pests you most likely will encounter can be easily eliminated, often via organic means. You will have the fewest problems with a collection that is cared for properly, but even the most conscientious gardener may encounter insect pests, especially during the winter months, when plants' defenses are at their lowest ebb. Another potential source of problems is a

new plant from an unfamiliar nursery. Err on the side of caution by isolating new arrivals for a week or two before placing them adjacent to your existing specimens. That way, if pests appear, you can deal with them before your entire collection is infested.

The insects that prey on indoor succulents include all the usual suspects plaguing other houseplants: aphids, spider mites, scale insects, and mealy bugs. These will most often appear when plants have recently been moved inside from outdoors, although they can also be brought in with new plants from the nursery, as mentioned. The stress of leaving the fresh air and sunshine on the balcony (or the greenhouse) and moving to the cooler, drier air and reduced light in front of a window can reduce plants' natural ability to resist pests. When this happens, otherwise insignificant pests can undergo a population explosion. Stressed plants are always the most likely targets for bugs.

Prevention being better than endeavoring to effect a cure, it is wise to take precautions just prior to bringing plants indoors. One of the best and simplest treatments for ridding your plants of insect hitchhikers is spraying them with insecticidal soap. This product is available from most garden centers and is harmless to plants, pets, and people. Do not substitute household soaps, as they may contain additional chemicals that could injure plants. Mix insecticidal soap with water according to the package directions. You can purchase a small sprayer at a garden center or get one for nothing when you buy a household product. I like to keep

an empty window cleaner spray bottle, which I have rinsed thoroughly, as a sprayer for my indoor plants. Choose a sunny, breezy day; spray the plants thoroughly; and allow them to dry off before moving them indoors.

Another good preventive treatment for your indoor succulents is neem oil. It smells somewhat like celery and is obtained from a tropical tree. Available at most well-stocked garden centers, neem oil is diluted with water before use. It can stain the foliage of some plants. I therefore recommend trying it on a small spot before you commit to wholesale coverage of a valued specimen.

If you discover that a plant has become infested with insects despite your best efforts, first isolate it from the rest of your collection. This will help to confine the outbreak. If only a small number of insects are present, the easiest remedy may be to kill them individually with a cotton swab dipped in rubbing alcohol. This treatment, although tedious, is highly effective against mealy bugs and scale insects. The alcohol penetrates the protective coatings these insects secrete around themselves, and then kills them. Spraying with insecticidal soap or neem oil may quell the infestation, depending upon the exact pest attacking your plant.

Aphids can often be eliminated simply by giving the plants a good dousing under the shower. A strong jet of water will knock most of the aphids off the plant, and down the drain they will go. Insecticidal soap is also effective against them.

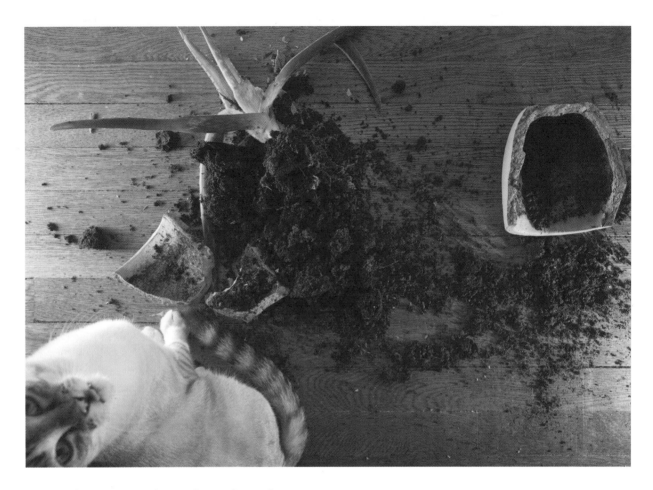

Most succulents can survive damage if repotted promptly

Spider mites, typically recognizable only by the tiny wisps of web that they spin on the undersurface of the plant's leaves or stems, often appear when the humidity is too low. They respond well to a treatment with insecticidal soap. Providing good air circulation around the plants and misting them now and then will help keep mites from returning.

If you do not object to the use of chemical insect controls, you can purchase systemic houseplant insecticide products containing imidocloprid. Sold as granules, the product is simply sprinkled on the surface of the potting mix prior to adding any mulch. Plants take up the product each time they are watered. It renders the entire plant toxic to pests. Do not use imidocloprid where children or pets might ingest the plants. Otherwise, few treatments are as effective against so wide a range of houseplant bugs.

Thankfully, succulents are far less susceptible to pest problems than are most other houseplants. You are more likely to have problems related to damage, either visible or unseen. Unseen damage usually involves the roots. A plant that remains too wet for too long or at the wrong time of year may develop root rot. This can advance, undetected, to the point that the plant suddenly collapses or wilts. With many succulents, you can simply lop off the entire root mass, allow the cut surface to air dry for a couple of days, and reroot the plant. (See the chapter on propagating succulents for recommendations on how to do this with various types of plants, page 53.)

Damage can also result from physical injury. One of the most common injuries is sunburn. This may seem nonsensical for plants that in their natural habitat are sometimes exposed to the harshest radiation imaginable, but it happens. Typically, the plant has spent a long winter in relative darkness and is moved out into bright sunshine without a gradual period of acclimation. Sunburned spots will turn yellow or brown and become watery (see photo, page 30). The remedy is simple. First, get the plant into a shadier spot. Second, use a sharp knife to excise the damage, cutting into the healthy tissue around the burn. Allow the cut to dry for a day or two, and then begin to gradually return the plant to sunny conditions over a period of a week to 10 days. On the first day, you might only leave the plant in the sun for one or two hours in the morning before moving it back to the shade.

Physical damage can also occur when plants are around kids, pets, or clumsy adults like me. I am always amazed at how my plants can recover after, say, falling from a shelf and crashing on the patio pavement. Seldom is the plant a total loss. If an accident happens to one of your plants, simply repot if needed, cut off the damaged portions, and allow the plant to recover. Sometimes such a mishap forces you to propagate a plant you hadn't planned on propagating. Anything you cut off of most succulents can usually be used to start a new plant. See the section on propagation for ideas.

See Chapter 4 for ideas on designing with and displaying your succulent collection. Regardless of the way you choose to display it, a collection of succulents can brighten up your indoor space, bringing a touch of the natural world to the built environment. And because their needs are few, you can care for a large number of potted succulents in only an hour or two each week.

CHAPTER 3

Propagating Succulents

If, like many houseplant enthusiasts, you find succulents to be fun and easy to grow, you will eventually want to increase your collection. One way to do that, of course, is to purchase more plants, but most of us avoid spending money needlessly. Fortunately, succulents are among the easiest of plants to propagate vegetatively. Leaf cuttings from echeverias, for example, are ready to pot up just a couple of months after they are removed from the parent plant. Several methods can be used that should permit you to propagate any of the plants in your collection.

Vegetative Propagation

By far the most common method for propagating succulents is vegetative propagation. This term refers to any form of propagation that does not involve sowing seeds and growing them to maturity. In practice, vegetative propagation can take many forms, from rooting stem and leaf cuttings to laboratory-based tissue culture. The most complicated techniques are best reserved for commercial production of plants that are otherwise difficult or impossible to propagate, but the simple ones can be carried out on your potting bench or kitchen table. Regardless of the exact method employed, vegetative propagation results in new plants that are genetically identical to their parents. In the case of some hybrids that do not produce seeds, vegetative methods are the only ones available to obtain additional plants.

PLANTLETS AND OFFSETS

Some succulents do all the propagation work for you, and obtaining new plants is child's play. For example, some *Kalanchoe* species produce plantlets along the leaf margins. Simply detaching one of these miniature replicas of the parent and giving it its own pot is all that is necessary. In areas where these plants are winter hardy, they have actually become pests due to their proclivity to propagate themselves. If you want to use this method, wait until roots are apparent on the plantlets, then dislodge them carefully from the parent.

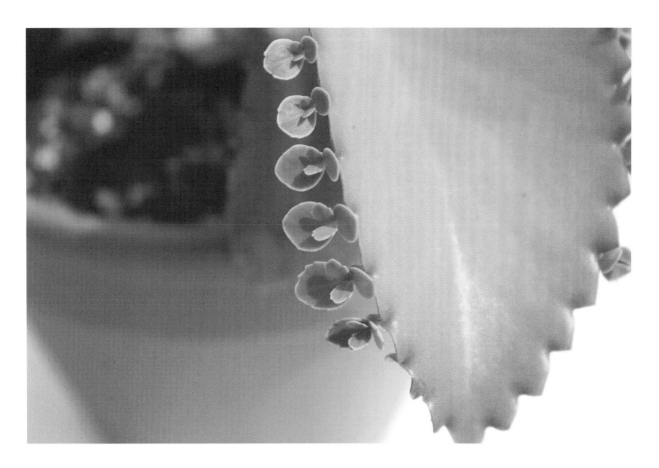

Numerous rosette-forming succulents and many cacti form offsets. These are miniature plants borne at the base of the parent, or they may be produced on short stems. Offsets are easily detached and rooted. Those that form on a stem can be cut free with a half-inch or more of stem attached. Insert the stem in a hole poked in a pot of growing medium, and roots will form in a couple of weeks. Offsets that do not grow from a stem can usually be separated from the parent by twisting and pulling gently. Many cacti have offsets like this. They are then rooted as described under *Methods for Cacti* on page 64.

Step-by-Step: Propagation by Offsets

1. Remove the parent plant with offsets from its pot. The example in this case is a *Sempervivum*.

2. Carefully separate the root mass, keeping the parent plant and its roots more or less intact.

3. Using your fingers, separate the individual offsets with their small clusters of roots.

4. You should now have a number of individual offsets ready for replanting. Simply fill pots with growing medium, pop in one of the offsets, water, and set aside. They should show signs of growth after a week or two.

LEAF CUTTINGS

Plants with leaves that come away from the stem readily are obvious candidates for propagation by leaf cuttings. Indeed, in many cases this is one way the population increases in the plant's natural habitat. For example, a passing animal might jostle leaves from a plant. These fall to the ground, in a few days produce roots, and eventually an entire new plant grows where the leaf landed. At home, this technique can be applied to a wide array of succulent varieties. Here are a few general rules:

- Detach leaves from obvious points of attachment along the stem. It should not be necessary to cut anything in order to remove a leaf.
- If the point of attachment exudes liquid to any significant degree, it is wise to allow the wound to heal before attempting to root the cutting. Simply place the cuttings on a tray and set them in a shady spot for 48 hours, then root them as described below.

Step-by-Step: Propagation by Leaf Cuttings

1. I poked holes in the bottom of this plastic tray from the grocery store before filling it with commercial potting mix for succulents.

2. Water the container thoroughly and allow it to drain well.

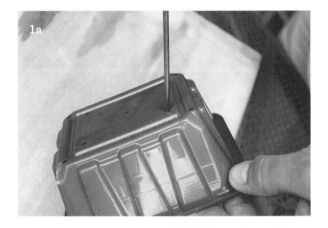

3. Remove one or more leaves from the plant you wish to propagate, in this case, an echeveria.

4. Place the leaves, curved side down, on the surface of the potting mix. Make sure the point where the leaf was attached to the plant is touching the soil. You can start as many cuttings as the container will accommodate without them touching.

5. Place the container with the cuttings where it will receive indirect light. Do not water or add fertilizer.

6. You should see new roots within 14 to 21 days, and a tiny new plant should form after about one week longer.

STEM CUTTINGS

The stem-cutting method of propagation lends itself to vining plants, such as sedums, but can also be used to propagate specimens whose leaves do not come loose easily. Treelike succulents, such as some *Crassula* species, respond well to this method. General rules are as follows:

- Use a sharp blade, not scissors or pruning shears, to remove cuttings from the parent plant. Try to slice the stem in one smooth motion. This minimizes damage to the vascular system, reducing the possibility of disease. The plant's vascular tissues can be crushed by scissors.
- As with leaf cuttings, stems that exude a lot of sap should be laid aside to dry for 48 hours before continuing with the procedure.

Step-by-Step: Propagation by Stem Cuttings

1. Fill a small pot with commercial potting mix for succulents.

2. Top the growing mix with sand.

3. Water the container thoroughly and allow it to drain well.

4. Remove stem sections from the plant you wish to propagate, in this case a sedum. Remove leaves from the cut end to expose a short section of stem.

5. Using a toothpick, bamboo skewer or other instrument, make a narrow hole in the potting mix and insert the stem of the cutting. Firm the soil gently around the stem. Repeat with additional cuttings, if using. Water the container, taking care not to dislodge the cutting.

6. Place the container with the cutting where it will receive indirect light. Do not water again or add fertilizer.

7. You should see new roots within 14 to 21 days. Leave them to grow for a month or more before transplanting.

METHODS FOR CACTI

Cacti can be propagated by offsets, which typically form at the base of mature plants. In some cases, cacti can be propagated by stem cuttings, provided the plant naturally branches in some way. A classic example of an easy cactus to propagate is *Mammillaria gracilis*, commonly known as "thimble cactus." It produces numerous offsets from the base of older ones. Older, larger portions of the plant may also develop smaller side branches. Any of these smaller growths can be detached whole and used to grow another plant.

Here is how to do it . . .

Step-by-Step: Cactus Cuttings

1. Here, I am propagating a clump of *Mammillaria gracilis*. Using tweezers, remove one of the offsets from the outer edge of the clump.

2. Have ready a small pot filled with your preferred growing mix. Make a shallow depression in the center of the growing mix.

3. Carefully place the offset into the depression in the pot.

4. Secure the offset in place with a pair of rubber bands. Water well, then set the pot aside in indirect light. The offset should root within a month.

ROOTING HORMONES

Plants that are reluctant to root from cuttings can often be induced to do so through the use of rooting hormones. Commercially available in both liquid and powder forms, these products contain natural plant hormones, such as indole-butyric acid (IBA), in various proportions. Dip cuttings briefly in one of these products, following the label directions, before placing them in a pot or tray to root as described previously.

Seed Propagation

Most of the commonly available succulents can be so easily propagated by vegetative means that growing them from seed, which is more exacting and takes longer to produce a mature plant, has almost been abandoned for some varieties. As a rule, however, you can grow a lot more plants from seed at a minimal cost. A packet of 100 seeds may cost the same as a single mature plant of the same species. Among the more popular and widely available seeds are those of cacti, which can be bought as individual species or, for the adventurous, as a mixed packet that may contain five or more types of seeds. For numerous other rare or unusually large succulents, seeds may be the only way an enthusiast can obtain plants. A quick online search will turn up numerous suppliers. Many of them offer detailed instructions for seed germination. These should be followed to the letter. As a general rule, seeds are sown on the

same potting mix used for mature plants, but the mix is screened to a finer texture. Prior to sowing, some seeds may need special treatment, such as scarification (physically damaging the seed coat to allow moisture in) or stratification (exposing the seed to a period of cold), before they will germinate. After sowing, some seeds may germinate rapidly, while others may take weeks. Because it is impossible to give complete instructions for every species one might potentially encounter, we will leave the topic of seed propagation with one caveat for the beginning grower: Carefully study the requirements of any plant you contemplate growing this way, and be prepared for some failures.

Using Artificial Lighting

If you propagate succulents at home, sooner or later you will find yourself running out of windows. This can also happen if you merely become an enthusiastic collector. However, you can turn even a dark closet into a home for succulents by using artificial lighting. Improvements in lighting technology make growing plants under lights easier and cheaper than ever before. To help you decide if artificial lighting might be useful in your situation, here are some basic lighting facts.

HOW MUCH LIGHT?

Sunlight is the energy source that drives photosynthesis. All plants, with the exception of some

unusual ones that have lost their green chlorophyll, require light to survive and grow. As most of us learn in elementary school, sunlight is composed of many different colors, or wavelengths, of light, from the invisible ultraviolet responsible for suntans to the invisible infrared that warms your skin on a sunny day. In between is the visible spectrum, some of which is utilized by plants. To a plant, all colors are not equal. Plants absorb light primarily in two regions of the spectrum, blue and red, as can be seen in the accompanying graphic.

To compare different light sources in terms of their suitability for plant growth, scientists have devised a measure known as "photosynthetically active radiation," or PAR. Simply stated, this is a measure of the amount of energy provided by a

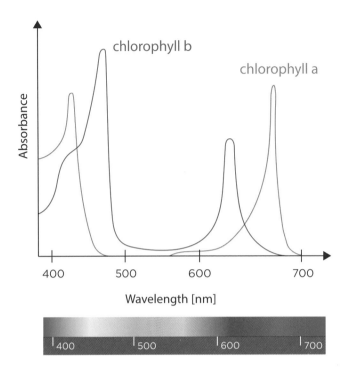

light source in those wavelengths of importance to plant growth. Measurement of PAR values must be carried out using an electronic instrument. This presents an inconvenience to the home gardener, as the devices are expensive, but fortunately many lighting manufacturers now provide PAR output information with regard to their products. For growing succulents, a PAR value of at least 100 units, measured 12 inches below the light source, is the minimum I would bother with. More is better, as outdoor sunshine can be many times greater than this. Light shade outdoors, for example, is typically around 200 PAR units.

How we humans perceive light has little to do with how plants respond to it. As a result, a light source that seems very bright may in fact not be the best choice for plant growth. The wattage, Kelvin temperature, and lumen output of a given light source, all of which are commonly available numbers, are of little use in determining the suitability of that light source for horticulture. Unfortunately, recommendations based on these values remain common in writing about growing plants. For example, Kelvin temperature measures how the lamp compares to "natural daylight" in terms of rendering colors, not its emission spectrum or PAR value. Nevertheless, "daylight" sounds like it might be good for plants, and this information makes its way into the literature as a recommendation. If you are unable to find PAR values for the equipment you are considering, your best bet is to provide as much light as is feasible in your situation. Most light sources generate some useful radiation for plants. The best sources for detailed lamp output data will be the lamp manufacturer's website. You can usually find the manufacturer's name and the lamp model number somewhere on the lamp itself. Manufacturer websites may provide an emission spectrum for the lamp you are researching. You can gain a rough idea of how this lamp will perform by comparing its emission spectrum to the chlorophyll absorption spectrum presented in the accompanying graphic. The more congruent the two curves are, the better the lamp will perform for plant growth.

FLUORESCENT LIGHTING

Fluorescent lighting has been around for a long time. In terms of cost, availability, and ease of use, this type of lighting may be your best choice, although the intensity of light output is relatively low. An inexpensive fixture available at any hardware or big-box store can be used for starting cuttings or to supplement the light from a window. Vendors that cater to home gardeners may offer fluorescent systems complete with supports, shelves, and other conveniences that make artificial light gardening easy. The biggest drawback to all of these systems is their often inadequate light output, meaning that plants must be no more than a few inches away from the lamps, or else many lamps must be used over a small area. This puts a severe limitation on the size of plants that such systems can accommodate. Fluorescent lighting systems are thus better for propagation than for maintaining a diverse collection of larger, more mature specimens.

METAL HALIDE LIGHTING

Commercial facilities growing plants indoors often use metal halide lighting, sometimes referred to as halogen quartz iodide (HQI) or high-intensity discharge (HID) lighting. This extremely bright form of incandescent lighting is undeniably effective but has some significant drawbacks when considered for use at home. The first issue is heat; metal halide lamps generate a lot of it. Forced air ventilation is usually necessary to prevent the growing area from becoming too warm. In addition, the added heat will increase the demand for air conditioning in summer.

Protecting metal halide lamps from being splashed with water, definitely a possibility in a growing space, is essential. The lamps operate at a very high temperature. Cold water reaching the hot glass can cause an explosion.

Another obvious concern is that small children and pets are clearly incompatible with such a lighting system.

Beyond safety considerations, metal halide lamps, although more efficient than fluorescent lamps, nevertheless consume a lot of electricity for the amount of photosynthetically active radiation they emit. If you are planning on a large space for an artificial light garden, this may be the way to go, but

I would urge you to carefully research the subject before you make a significant investment.

LED LIGHTING
The future of artificial lighting for most purposes is the light-emitting diode, or LED. This solid-state device combines efficiency, small size, and ready availability in lighting systems that are customized for everything from makeup mirrors to television production, and units designed for plant growth are now widely available. Because LEDs can be precisely "tuned" to emit light of a desired wavelength, units can be manufactured that have high PAR values while simultaneously being extremely energy efficient. Some of the LEDs designed specifically for plant growth emit a pur-

ple glow because they produce only the red and blue wavelengths that plants use. While this is fine for production purposes, people who want to display plants at home may prefer a light source that looks more natural. These types of LED systems exist and are widely available.

The aquarium industry has been creating LED lighting systems that support freshwater plants and photosynthetic marine organisms for a while now. If you go shopping for an aquarium tank to use as a terrarium (terrariums are discussed in the following chapter) you are likely to find one outfitted with a plant growth–enhancing LED light strip. These are a good investment, and experience indicates that the plants grow like crazy. Aquarium equipment is also, of course, moisture resistant.

There are two drawbacks to consider with regard to LED lighting. First, the equipment may be more expensive than other types of lighting systems that deliver the same PAR value. This initial cost, however, can be offset by savings in electricity costs over the life of the unit. That depends on where you live and how much you pay for your utilities, of course. Second, LED lighting units typically have a life span of about 10 years when used for plant production at 8 to 12 hours per day of "on" time. Therefore, the initial cost, when amortized over the life of the unit, is relatively small. When making comparisons, one must also consider the cost of replacement lamps for fluorescent and metal halide systems. Fluorescent lamps should be replaced annually, while metal halide lamps remain useful for up to three years before their light output

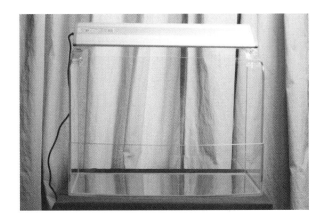

Above and opposite: LED lights

becomes too low to maintain peak plant growth. Unlike fluorescent or metal halide lamps, which can be replaced, LEDs must be discarded or recycled at the end of their useful life. Their compactness, energy efficiency, and light output should outweigh these negatives for many houseplant hobbyists, however.

Even if you don't want to develop a huge collection, propagating your plants can be a fun activity that the entire family can enjoy. It would not take an especially creative person to devise plant propagating projects that will engage children. Many succulents root and establish themselves so quickly that even an impatient child can achieve relatively fast results. If you have room and a suitable light source, you can propagate most succulents by one of the methods outlined in this chapter.

Now let us consider some ways in which you can display your growing collection.

CHAPTER 4

Designing with Succulents

Succulents lend themselves to all sorts of arrangements. Even though your primary growing space is indoors, you will be able to adorn your home with a remarkably wide variety of plants. Your main limitation will be the amount of lighted space you have available for your succulent collection, whether the illumination comes from the sun or from artificial lighting. Apart from that restriction, succulents can be displayed in any room in the house and will enhance any decor.

Achieving a Natural Look

Some people like to create miniature succulent landscapes that closely approximate how the plant would appear if it were growing in its natural habitat. When succulent enthusiasts get together to compete for the most beautifully grown container plants, the "natural" approach to container design is the one that usually receives the most attention. While the exceptional specimens achieved by home gardeners are partly the result of having an eye for design and a skilled hand at arranging plants, they are also the result of paying attention to some basic principles. You can easily learn to employ the same principles in designing your own indoor succulent gardens. These principles are: symmetry, rhythm, balance, and character. Let's take a moment to explore what each of these implies in terms of your designs.

Symmetry in a design results from repeating the same element more than once in the composition. When we think about symmetry, we may first think about the arrangement of similar elements around a central point, as in a starfish. But symmetry also lies in arranging similar elements in other ways. Three individuals of the same species planted together produce symmetry, especially if they are all the same size. The individual plants may be arranged in a triangle, implying a central axis, or evenly spaced along a straight line. Either arrangement is symmetrical. An arrangement featuring multiple plants always looks more "natural" than a single plant standing alone in a pot. Multiples can all be in the same pot or in individual ones. As a subsidiary rule, odd numbers of items, whether they are plants or rocks, look more natural than even numbers. When elements are repeated in even-numbered multiples, the resulting design takes on a "formal" look. Compare a Victorian knot garden (formal) with a Japanese strolling garden (natural), and you can quickly discern the operation of this principle on a grand scale. The eye is drawn to symmetrical arrangements of objects. If you want a striking focal point, maintain its symmetry for maximum effectiveness.

Rhythm creates a feeling of movement and brings the element of time into the fabric of the design. Planting three individuals of the same species, but of different sizes and ages, suggests the inevitable progress from youth to old age. Three otherwise identical pots of proportionately different sizes draws attention to the ascending or descending scale of the arrangement. The presentation is symmetrical but is far more interesting than if all the plants were the same size. Such variation is what we consistently find in nature. If a natural look is not what you want, create a sense of formality by incorporating repeated elements that are all the same size, and inject rhythm by choosing containers in different, but harmonious, colors.

The principle of rhythm also applies to non-living components of the design, such as rocks. Three rocks of varying size but from the same material convey a "natural" feel, while three nearly identical rocks would seem formal, more like a sculpture.

Balance is achieved through harmonious combinations of color and form. Thus, the color of the container might be mirrored in the foliage color of the plants within it. Or a tall, columnar, spiky cactus is balanced by the inclusion of a smooth, rounded stone beside it in the pot. This latter placement would also keep the cactus out of the center of the pot, avoiding an "upside-down lollipop" effect. Displaying taller plants in tall pots also helps to alleviate this effect.

One might also achieve balance with a mixed planting. A low-growing rosette of *Echeveria elegans* might be paired with the fuzzy, upright stems and foliage of *Kalanchoe tomentosa*. The smooth, cool look of the echeveria is balanced by the rough, warm-toned appearance of the

kalanchoe. As a rule, fine-textured plants are balanced by coarsely textured ones, and low, spreading forms are balanced by either rosettes or columnar shapes. For larger containers, columnar, rosette, and spreading plant shapes can all work together to create a balanced, harmonious display. Nonliving materials can be included in the arrangement as a substitute for one of these forms. For example, a rounded stone could replace a squat miniature cactus, or a branch of driftwood could stand in for a columnar plant. Take care, however,

not to add too many diverse elements in a single design. The smaller the pot, the fewer elements it can accommodate without looking cluttered.

Character can apply to the entire arrangement or just some aspect of it. When I think of character in a design, I also think of the Japanese principle of *wabi sabi*, which celebrates the value of traits such as imperfection and transience. Thus, an old, cracked container that is nevertheless still serviceable has more character than a brand-new pot. Within the concept of character lies the appeal

of found or repurposed objects that often bear the scars of their history.

When applied to a complete planting, character might flow from the gnarled appearance of the trunk of a large, mature crassula plant. Scars left behind after damage heals can bring character to a plant, too. Succulents are survivors. Nothing implies this more strongly than a plant that has recovered from damage. Formality in the character of an arrangement can be implied by the use of

new, shiny materials as opposed to older, weathered ones for containers. This is the opposite of wabi sabi, but nevertheless has its place in some settings. Minimalist modern decorating themes might call for this type of formality in presentation, for example.

By thinking about and applying these elements to your own designs for succulent container gardens, you will be able to create aesthetically pleasing indoor gardens that reflect nature. A carefully chosen group of individual plants in containers can capture these elements as well as a mixed planting in a single container. Most importantly, your designs should reflect your personal preferences, aesthetic, and imagination. You are the final arbiter of design in your living space.

Mixed Succulent Container Gardens

Mixed container gardens featuring a variety of succulents enjoy huge popularity, based on their ubiquitous appearance just about anywhere you might expect to see live plants for sale. Succulent combinations turn up in terrariums, in planters, and in whimsical containers such as toy trucks. Because succulents can go for long periods without growing too much, mixed container gardens last a long time before they need to be broken down and replanted.

Creating an appealing mixed container of succulents requires little apart from a good eye. Follow the standard rule for creating a mixed planter of flowers: fill, spill, and thrill. You need a focal point plant for the "thrill," such as *Euphorbia tirucalli*. Include a low, mounding plant, such as *Euphorbia obesa*, for "fill," and a trailing or fine-textured plant, such as *Senecio rowleyanus*, for "spill." Don't forget to take into account the flowers that some succulents will readily produce when they receive sufficient light. Succulent flowers are often borne in spikes or sprays that will arch away from the main planting,

toward the sun, adding rhythm and a spot of color to the display.

Succulents from the far-flung corners of the planet may be grouped together in a single container planting. In such cases, the designer has maximum flexibility in choosing the color and form of the plants. For those who like a slightly more challenging approach, try creating mixed plantings using only plants that would be found together in their natural habitats. Fortunately, the many varieties of succulents available commercially tend to come from comparatively few regions, making the task of selection easier. Numerous crassulas and euphorbias, for example, are found in South Africa, as are the kalanchoes. Cacti, on the other hand, are mostly New World plants, as are the echeverias.

Don't forget to include rocks, wood, or other materials in your design. A striking piece of weathered wood might serve the function of "thriller" just as well as a plant could do.

Other Indoor Designs

I have already alluded to the use of succulents to create wreaths, table decorations, and other variations on mixed plantings. These designs, in which the plants are arranged like cut flowers, do not last as long as typical container plantings, but they can be surprisingly durable. The purely decorative and temporary arrangements rely on a loose but water-retentive material such as sphagnum moss or coco-

nut fiber as the substrate into which the roots of the plants are placed. These designs generally do not receive fertilization, as the goal is to keep the plants alive but not necessarily growing.

Succulent wreath arrangements are typically built using a wire form available at florist supply shops. The form is packed with damp sphagnum moss, and succulent cuttings are inserted to create the design. The wreath is laid flat for a few weeks to allow the plants to take root, after which time it can be hung up for display. These arrangements need watering about once every 10 days to two weeks when kept indoors.

Succulents mounted in a vertical frame have enjoyed increasing popularity. For this type of arrangement to work, the root balls of the succulents are placed in a shallow box of standard growing mix that is enclosed in a frame. Wire or plastic mesh holds the growing mix in place. Such designs can last more than one growing season with proper attention to care. It is necessary to allow the arrangement to grow horizontally for about a month after planting for the plants to secure themselves in place with their roots. After that, the frame can be placed on a wall for display like a framed print.

Step-by-Step: Creating a Succulent Wreath

1. You will need a wreath frame, florist wire, utility scissors, and sphagnum moss for this project, in addition to the plants.

2. Choose a selection of plants that suits your fancy. Echeverias and sedums work well for wreath making.

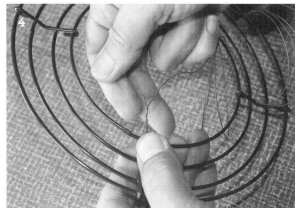

3. Soak the sphagnum moss in water for about 10 minutes before you begin filling the wreath frame.

4. Attach one end of a long piece of florist wire to the wreath frame by wrapping it around one of the frame wires several times.

5. Take a handful of the soaked sphagnum and squeeze out most of the water. Stuff the damp sphagnum into the wreath frame near where you attached the florist wire. Wrap the wire around the moss to secure it in place.

Continued

6. Continue adding sphagnum moss to the frame, working your way around and wrapping florist wire around the moss to hold it, until you have completely filled the frame. Wrap the free end of the florist wire around a frame wire a few times to secure it, then cut off any excess. The wreath is now ready for planting.

7. Plant the wreath by inserting the root balls into the sphagnum moss. If you use sedums, you can plant cuttings 2 to 3 inches in length. Use a pair of tweezers to assist you, if necessary.

8. When planting echeverias, remove some leaves from the stem, then make an opening in the moss with a toothpick. Insert the stem into the opening.

9. Space plants to allow room for them to grow. The finished wreath will look much better if the plants grow in naturally. When finished planting, place the wreath on a tray and mist thoroughly. Leave the wreath to lie flat for two to three weeks, after which time the plants should have rooted into the sphagnum moss. Mist every few days, or soak the entire wreath in water for five minutes, then drain thoroughly.

TABLE DECORATIONS

Table decorations can be made using many of the same materials as wreaths, but the range of designs can be much broader. Fill any suitable decorative container with pots of several small succulents, then cover the spaces between them with Spanish moss, reindeer moss, or similar items. Or, fill a decorative cachepot with dampened sphagnum moss, add several succulents, and mulch the top with pebbles. Table decorations can include cut flowers, evergreen branches, fruits, vegetables, or other materials with a short life span. You may want to incorporate a block of florist foam into the design if you use cut flowers, as the sphagnum may not provide adequate moisture to keep them looking fresh.

SUCCULENT FRAME DISPLAYS

Another interesting and popular design featuring succulents is the "picture frame." A shallow tray holding the growing medium is surrounded with a decorative wood frame. Typically, plastic or wire mesh is placed over the growing medium to hold it in place when the frame is placed vertically. An assortment of succulents is planted within the confines of the frame to create a living "image." When well executed, these can be some of the most attractive displays of succulent diversity. The frame can take on the look of an aerial photograph if one uses their imagination.

For your first attempt at creating such a display, I recommend purchasing a ready-made frame or kit. Attempt to construct the whole thing from scratch only if you have significant handyman skills and the necessary tools. I found that a ready-made kit was also no more expensive than the materials I would need, with the added bonus of no labor to assemble the frame. I have included basic instructions for doing this project from scratch after the step-by-step.

Step-by-Step: Creating a Succulent "Picture"

For a small display, limit yourself to three to five varieties of plants. Use one, three, or five individual plants of each variety you select. You may also want to incorporate a creeping variety, such as a sedum, to fill in the spaces between the main plantings. Alternatively, you can use florist moss, as I have done in this example. I purchased a ready-made frame constructed of western red cedar online. It is slightly smaller than 1-foot square and will require about 6 to 10 plants to fill, depending upon which plants are chosen. Besides the frame itself and the plants, you will need a bag of your favorite succulent potting mix; a plastic utility tub or dish pan; a pair of wire cutters, scissors, or a sharp knife; and your choice of "filler" to go between the plants. If you use florist moss, as I did, you may need a small amount of florist wire to secure some pieces in place. You can find all these materials online, at your favorite craft store, or at a big-box retailer.

The frame itself is made from western red cedar, grooved at one edge to hold the wire mesh and on the opposite edge to accommodate a panel of quarter-inch concrete board. The concrete board is secured in place by a metal clip and can be removed or replaced as one wishes. Inside the frame, behind

the mesh, is a layer of porous landscape fabric. When you are ready to plant, remove the back panel and fill the space with growing mix. Replacing the back panel keeps the growing mix in place when you turn the frame over. Insert the plants through both the wire mesh and the porous fabric, cutting them as needed to make way for the root ball. When the frame is ready to hang, the back panel will protect the wall behind the frame from moisture and keep the growing mix in place. Two holes drilled in what becomes the bottom side of the frame provide drainage when the frame is mounted vertically.

2a

2b

2c

2d

1. In a utility tub, moisten a sufficient amount of your preferred succulent potting mix with water until it is evenly moist but not soggy. For this example, about a gallon of potting mix will be required. Water all of the plants thoroughly and allow them to drain for 10 or 15 minutes while you fill the frame with potting mix.

2. Place the frame mesh side down and remove the back panel. Fill the frame with potting mix, pressing it down firmly, but not too tightly, as you will need room for the root balls of the plants. Replace the back panel and flip the frame over with the mesh up.

Continued

3. Arrange the plants, still in their pots, on the top of the wire mesh. Try different arrangements until you are happy with the result. Changes are easy at this point but become more difficult as the project takes form. Try to imagine how the arrangement will look when the plants have grown for a month or two. That will be when your picture is ready to hang. When you are satisfied with your arrangement, you might want to snap a photo or two with your phone to help you duplicate the design when you do the actual planting.

4. Beginning at one corner of the frame, prepare to install the plants according to the photos you took. Gently remove each plant from its pot. Allow any excess potting mix to fall away from the root ball. Try to avoid damaging too many roots, but it is helpful if the root ball is as small as feasible.

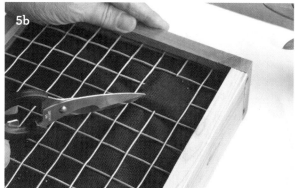

5. Start planting in one corner of the frame. Using wire cutters, remove portions of the mesh, as needed, to accommodate the root ball. Similarly, cut an opening in the porous fabric. Beginning with the larger ones, make a hole in the growing mix and insert the root ball. Firm the mix around the base of the plant. Use a stick or the handles of the wire cutter to help tamp the growing mix in place, if necessary.

Continued

6. Continue adding plants according to your planned design until you have filled the frame to your satisfaction. Cut away wire and fabric as needed, always aiming for the smallest opening that will accommodate the plant's roots.

7. When all the plants are in place, fill in the spaces between them with your preferred "filler" material, in this case florist moss. If necessary, use florist wire to secure the moss to the wire mesh in the frame.

8. Water the arrangement thoroughly by placing it in a sink or other location where water won't be an issue. Give it a gentle soaking with the sink sprayer or use a spray bottle of water. Excess water will find its way out. Leave the frame on a horizontal surface for three to four weeks to allow the plants to form roots and secure themselves in the growing mix. Water whenever the growing mix is almost completely dried out, or once a week, whichever comes first. Use a spray bottle to mist

each plant thoroughly. Make sure the frame is receiving bright, indirect light during this time.

9. Once the plants have grown securely into the frame, it can be mounted on a wall like a picture or set vertically on a high shelf. Pay attention to the moisture level in the growing mix and water the frame well when it is almost dried out. Add a balanced, soluble fertilizer at half the manufacturer's recommended strength to the water once every two months. Weak fertilization will help keep the plants looking healthy, while restraining them from outgrowing the frame.

DOING IT YOURSELF

If you have the tools and skills, you can make a succulent frame in any size you desire. This is a particularly good way to use an old picture frame found at a flea market, but of course you can always purchase one. Select your frame first, as its dimensions will determine everything else about the construction.

The finished succulent frame, ready to plant, consists of the following parts: the decorative outer frame, a piece of wire or plastic mesh that fills the space in the frame where glass would be in a picture, and a water-resistant, shallow box that fits behind the mesh to contain the growing medium that will support the succulent plants. If the frame you select is not weather resistant and you intend to display the arrangement outdoors, it is necessary to give it a coat of either exterior paint or a clear exterior finish if you wish to preserve the finish already on the frame. The box should be constructed of weather-resistant cedar and exterior-grade plywood, or it will be necessary to apply a water-resistant finish to these elements as well.

Once you have the frame you like and have protected its finish against the weather, if necessary, measure carefully and build the wooden box just slightly larger than the opening in the frame. Western red cedar 1-by-3-inch furring strips come in various lengths and are a good choice for this project. Use quarter-inch exterior plywood or concrete board for the bottom of the box. Cut the plywood to the size determined by your measurements and double-check to make sure it covers the opening in the frame appropriately. Cut four pieces of the cedar to surround the edges of the plywood, forming a shallow box. When you are certain of the fit, assemble these pieces at their corners with small nails. Coat the edges of the box with wood glue, lay the plywood in place on top of that, and attach the plywood with nails driven at intervals around the perimeter. If you are using concrete board, you will need to attach it with screws rather than nails.

Give some thought to how you will attach the box to the decorative frame. For anything larger than about 12 inches square, use a combination of glue and screws to hold the parts together. Smaller assemblies can rely on glue alone. First, line up the box and frame precisely. Mark the location of the box corners with a pencil to guide you when assembling. Use 8-by-2-inch flat-head wood screws through the edges of the box and into the back of the frame. Using an extra-long ⅛-inch bit, drill a pilot hole all the way through the plywood and box, and slightly into the back of the outer frame. Next, choose a drill bit slightly larger than the diameter of the screw head and drill a countersink 1¼ inches into the bottom edges of the box. (That is, through the plywood and 1 inch into the 1-by-3.) You need at least two screws per edge for a secure fit. Use more depending upon the dimensions of the assembly. Screws should be placed about 1 foot apart. Start the screws in their holes, allowing the point to protrude slightly.

Galvanized hardware cloth with a 1-inch mesh is a suitable material for this project, but for greater ease of cutting, not to mention fewer fingers poked by sharp edges, opt for black polypropylene hardware cloth with a similar mesh size. This material is usually sold for garden fencing and comes in rolls. Look for the smallest roll you can find, or else plan to make multiple frames. Locating a reasonable quantity of this or the galvanized material proved to be the greatest difficulty encountered when I went shopping for materials for a project like this. That is why I recommend purchased frame kits for smaller installations. Regardless of the material selected, cut a piece of the mesh to fit the opening in your decorative frame. Lay it in place and staple it firmly with a heavy-duty staple gun.

Finally, assemble the frame to the box. Run a bead of carpenter's glue around the perimeter of the box. Carefully flip it over, position the screws in their respective pilot holes, and tighten them all securely. Wipe away any excess glue with a damp cloth. Leave the assembly to dry for 24 hours before you fill it with growing mix. To fill and plant the frame, follow the instructions for smaller frames previously given, except simply fill the frame with lightly moistened growing mix from the front, pushing it through the wire mesh.

If you wish to duplicate the frame I purchased, you will need a table saw to cut the grooves in the material to hold the removable back and the mesh. This is a project for a skilled woodworker, and I will not offer additional instructions here. If you have the tools and the skills, your best bet is to examine one of the commercial models to see how it could be duplicated.

TERRARIUMS

Terrariums, usually thought of as mixed plantings enclosed in glass, can be death chambers for succulents. Too tight an enclosure will raise humidity to levels conducive to fungal growth. Soil moisture will remain high, leading to root rot. Sunshine becomes not the power of life but the instrument of death when trapped under glass. Thus, the foremost requirement for an arid terrarium is that it either be open-topped or have fan-forced ventilation. Obviously, the former is cheaper and easier and will be our method of choice for this example.

We must also be cautious about our choice of growing medium. Terrariums do not lend themselves to the sharp drainage that most succulents require. Accordingly, using a completely inert mixture of pebbles, coarse sand or gravel, and calcined clay is recommended. You can also use your favorite growing mix, but be sure to place a drainage layer of pebbles underneath it, as I do in the accompanying example.

Because of its capacity to retain water, a terrarium will likely require even less frequent care than a group of plants growing in a pot. As the intention when growing plants in a terrarium is to keep the plants somewhat restrained in their ability to fill all the available space, only an occasional application of fertilizer is needed. Thus, a well-designed succulent terrarium can be almost maintenance-free.

A cleverly done terrarium conveys a sense of microcosm, a world in miniature. If illuminated with an artificial light source, the terrarium brings a bit of nature to any corner of the home, even where no natural sunlight is available. For this example, I am using a large glass container, and the terrarium will be placed in a sunny window. The key to success, as always, is choosing the right plants. Select varieties that naturally remain relatively small so they won't quickly grow out of proportion to the container. Good choices include some of the weird forms that have been selected by nurseries over the years, as they are typically slow growing compared to their normal-looking parents. The finger jade plant, *Crassula ovata* 'Gollum,' is a good example, as is *Sempervivum* 'Oddity.' Other choices include *Adromischus cristatus*, *Haworthia* cultivars, and various sedums.

Step-by-Step: Creating a Terrarium

1 Begin by placing a layer of pebbles in the bottom of the container. This will create a drainage space that you can inspect periodically to determine if the terrarium needs watering or should be left to dry out further.

2 Spread a layer of growing medium on top of the pebbles.

3. If your terrarium is to be a large and complicated installation, you should arrange the plants, still in their pots, on a work surface or even in the terrarium itself, rearranging them until you are happy

with the design. You may want to take some photos at this point to allow you to re-create your design when you transplant the succulents into the terrarium container. For this simple design, I will plant the largest plant first, followed by successively smaller ones.

4. Unpot and place each plant where you want it, beginning with the largest plant and continuing with successively smaller ones, ending with the ground cover, if you are using one. As you go,

fill in around the root balls with more growing medium. Make sure plants are firmly in place so they won't topple before they have grown new roots into the medium.

If you are including larger rocks or other objects in the design, add them at this point, pressing them part of the way into the growing medium. They look more natural if partially covered.

5. When all plants are in place, finish off the display with a mulch of sand, pebbles, or a combination.

6. Water the growing medium sparingly, using a spray bottle or small watering can, just until a little water accumulates in the bottom layer of pebbles. Capillary action will help carry water to the surface as the medium dries out.

7. Carefully clean the inside of the glass to eliminate excess moisture and any stray flecks of potting mix.

8. Set the terrarium in bright, indirect light for a week or two to allow the plants to recover from transplanting, then move it to its permanent position near a sunny window. Water only when the medium is dry to a depth of one inch.

As you gain experience in growing these incredibly adaptable plants, you will no doubt develop numerous designs of your own. This is one of the most pleasurable aspects of working with succulents.

CHAPTER 5

Succulents to Grow

The world of succulents is vast and diverse, and I could not possibly list and describe every one of the approximately 2,000 species in the space I have. I have endeavored to select some representative examples of multiple succulent groups and have arranged them in what I believe to be a logical manner from the point of view of a hobbyist who wants to start a collection with a few plants on the windowsill, and perhaps move up to more challenging or larger plants when space and budget allow.

SUCCULENTS

Succulents for Beginners

This group contains the hardiest and least demanding plants in the book. As a rule, they will tolerate varying levels of lighting, indoor levels of humidity and temperature, and benign neglect. As with any of the other species described, these plants fare least well when overwatered or when potted in a medium that retains too much moisture. Given optimal amounts of light, moisture, and fertilizer, they may grow with surprising rapidity but will respond to less-than-ideal circumstances with no symptom more alarming than slow or no growth.

Aloe vera: This is the classic medicinal aloe. It grows easily given bright, indirect light and a well-drained growing medium. Water only when the soil is dry from spring to fall, and do not water at all in winter. During the growing season, feed with a half-strength commercial soluble fertilizer two or three times. Plants are capable of reaching 2 feet in diameter. The healing properties of the sap are well known. It can be applied to insect bites, minor burns, or scrapes for pain relief.

Beaucarnea recurvata: The "ponytail palm" is not a palm at all, but a member of the asparagus family. It is found in eastern Mexico and has been a popular houseplant likely because of the unique shape of its woody, succulent trunk, or "caudex," which is globular at the base and then tapers up to the cluster of strap-like leaves at the top. Ironically, natural populations of this easy-to-grow plant and its relatives are in trouble, mostly due to human encroachment on their habitat. Like other succulents, the crucial factor in cultivating them is to avoid overwatering. Take great care when repotting to avoid damage to the roots, but otherwise, the plants are tough, slow-growing houseplants that can live for years in the same pot. Specimens in the wild have been documented at more than 350 years of age. Feed plants once at the beginning of the growing season, using a balanced, soluble fertilizer, and give them plenty of sunshine.

Crassula ovata: Jade plant may well be the most commonly sold succulent. It is found in the eastern Cape region of South Africa and ranges northward from there. The same area is also home to a similar species, *C. arborescens.* The latter is superficially similar but grows much larger and has leaves that are silvery, rather than lime green as with *C. ovata.* Numerous cultivated forms of *C. ovata* exist, some with attractive red edging on the leaves when grown in bright sunshine. The cultivar 'Blue Surprise' has thinner, pointed leaves that cup slightly, and is a smoky blue color. Jade plants can easily reach 3 feet in height, and a well-grown specimen is among the most dramatic indoor trees that one might choose, with its handsome brown branches studded with leaves like smooth, green river stones. Like other trees, jade plants can be used to create interesting and beautiful bonsai via thoughtful pruning.

C. ovata grows with little to no attention from the gardener but with only the slightest coddling can become truly luxuriant. If you want a large specimen plant, repot regularly into a pot 2 inches wider in diameter than the previous one. Feed in spring when the weather warms up for the season. If you would rather keep your plant more compact, keep it in the same pot and prune the top growth. Withhold fertilizer unless the leaves begin to yellow. Any pruned-off stems can be rooted to form new plants. Plants that flop over are in desperate need of water. This usually happens when the roots are damaged by excessively wet potting mix or when the top growth becomes so large that the root mass is no longer sufficient to supply it with water. The remedy is to take the plant out of its pot, remove the old, decayed potting mix, and repot in a larger pot with fresh mix. Sometimes the branches will not straighten up by themselves and will require being

Clockwise from top left: Aloe vera, Beaucarnea recurvata, Crassula ovata *jade*, Crassula ovata *bonsai*

Clockwise from top left: Euphorbia trigona ‘*Rubra*,’ Euphorbia trigona, Euphorbia milii, Haworthia attenuata

tied to stakes to hold them in place. Once the plant is fully recovered, the stakes can be removed.

Euphorbia milii: Known all over the world as "crown of thorns," this Madagascar species is popular because of its free-flowering nature. Consisting of branching, woody stems that bear pairs of spines, the plant produces thin, flat leaves along the stems and flowers surrounded by bright scarlet bracts near the stem tips. The variety *imperatae* is a genetic dwarf that will be quite happy living in a 4-inch pot. Most places that stock succulents will have this plant.

Euphorbia trigona: Also known as "cathedral plant," *E. trigona* has graced student apartments for at least 40 years now. Botanists believe it originated in drier regions of India, but the plant is now so widespread, its precise origins are lost in the mists of time. It is among the easiest of all tree-like succulents to grow and is an ideal choice if you want a larger plant in a less-than-ideal spot. The stems are flattened on the sides, triangular in cross section, and are armed with short, dark spines. Thin, fingerlike leaves sprout from the ridges between the spines. Older plants begin to branch and can be encouraged to do so by removing the main growing point with a sharp knife. Eventually, this species will grow to 4 feet or more in height. Care is the same as for other euphorbias, although this one will tolerate shadier conditions and does not mind the potting mix drying out before it is watered again.

For the most impressive growth, repot every two years into a pot 2 inches larger in diameter than the previous one. The cultivar 'Rubra' has attractive, dark red leaves and dark red pigmentation in the stem. It grows more slowly than the species.

Haworthia attenuata: Undoubtedly because the white tubercles on the leaves create attractive patterns, the genus *Haworthia* is represented by dozens upon dozens of cultivated forms, most of which derive from this species. The leaves are stiff and sharp pointed. Although blooms may occur, most varieties produce offsets that are the source for the nursery stock you are likely to encounter. The native range is South Africa, with subgenera recognized on the basis of flower structure. Regardless of the taxonomy, all these plants do best in a potting mix that is less than 25 percent organic matter. Water monthly, less frequently in winter. I have seen plants remain in the same container for years without fertilization or repotting.

Kalanchoe tomentosa: Several cultivars of this species exist. The one pictured is a compact cultivar, 'Chocolate Soldiers.' Collectively, they are known as "panda plants." The fuzzy leaves of pale gray-green blotched with brown are characteristic. Try not to wet the leaves when watering, as this may encourage fungal growth. Allow the soil to dry out almost completely before rewatering, and give little to no water in winter. Repot in spring. Feed two weeks after repotting and twice more during the growing season.

Sansevieria cylindrica: Looking like a cluster of green spikes protruding from the soil, this species is native to Angola. Like its more commonly cultivated cousin, *S. trifasciata*, this species is durable and undemanding in cultivation. Give the plant a weekly watering in the growing season, monthly in winter. Do not feed in winter, but feed monthly during the warmer months. Although it grows well in bright light, this plant is more shade tolerant than many other succulents.

Sansevieria trifasciata: Commonly known as "snake plant" or "mother-in-law's tongue," this African native has been in cultivation for a very long time. As a result, numerous cultivated forms are available, most with attractive patterns of variegation, and a few with only stripes of green in otherwise white leaves. Some varieties have attractive, golden-yellow leaf margins. Legendary for its hardiness, snake plant will grow even in a shady corner, provided it does not get too much moisture. The plant likes "tight shoes." Repot only when root bound. Withhold both food and water during winter, but feed plants monthly with a weak solution of fer-

From left: Kalanchoe tomentosa, Sansevieria cylindrica, Sansevieria trifasciata

Echeveria *collection*

tilizer during the growing season. Best growth will occur in bright, but indirect, light.

Popular Groups of Succulents

I have placed in this category several groups of succulents that have found wide acceptance and that include numerous varieties. In addition to multiple wild species, these groups also feature many cultivars. This proliferation of varieties often leads hobbyists to assemble a collection of as many members of a single group as possible. Part of the popularity of these groups lies in their ease of culture. While most do best with proper care and adequate sun-

shine, a period of neglect or an error in watering need not spell disaster. Most of the time, a stressed plant will recover if the problem is promptly corrected after it is detected.

ECHEVERIAS

Among the most popular succulents, echeverias come in hundreds of species and cultivated varieties. So many species and forms of *Echeveria* exist, we would be hard pressed to cover them all in a book of this size. Create a beautiful display by grouping a selection of them in a sunny window. Use pots of various heights and widths, and plants of various sizes for a naturalistic grouping, or grow several of one plant in identical pots for a minimalist, modern look. The great thing about a collection of echeverias is that they all require similar growing conditions. Pot them in commercial potting mix made for cacti and succulents to which you have added 25 percent perlite, fine gravel, or coarse sand to provide sharper drainage. Keep them in bright light but out of direct sun in summer. In winter, give them a cool spot with as much sun as possible. Do not water the plants during winter dormancy, but water during the warmer months when the surface of the potting mix feels dry to the touch. Apply balanced liquid fertilizer at half the manufacturer's recommended strength when the weather warms up in spring and every six weeks thereafter until cool weather returns in late autumn. Happy plants will produce erect stems bearing red, pink, yellow, or orange flowers from late spring through summer. Do not be alarmed as lower leaves on otherwise healthy plants shrivel and die. This is a natural tendency for echeverias and will eventually result in a treelike structure with the rosettes of leaves at the ends of the branches. If this look does not appeal to you, simply cut off the rosettes with an inch of stem attached and insert the stem into a pot of growing mix. It will root, and the branch from which the rosette was removed will regrow one or more new rosettes. Impressive echeveria "bonsai" can be created in this fashion.

From top: Echeveria *'Aquarius'*, Echeveria elegans, Echeveria *'Gray Red'*

Echeveria 'Aquarius': An unusual and popular *Echeveria* cultivar, 'Aquarius' is slow growing but undemanding, as are most members of the genus. The crinkled, pale green leaves with pink edging add a whimsical note to mixed container plantings. Culture is the same as for other echeverias.

Echeveria elegans: This is one of the most popular and widely available echeverias, sporting pale bluish-green leaves with deep maroon edging. The flowers are pink and yellow. It produces offsets readily, to the delight of growers and hobbyists alike. Multiple cultivars also exist.

Echeveria 'Gray Red': This is a cultivar of *E. elegans* that has deep pink coloration on the undersides of the leaves in bright light. The rosette of leaves that is characteristic of the genus closes more tightly in bright light but is more lax in shadier circumstances. As with other echeverias, its only demands are sharp drainage and dappled sunshine.

Echeveria lilacina: The dusty coating on the leaves of this lovely *Echeveria* gives it a purplish glow. Native to the drier regions of northeastern Mexico, it is as amenable to cultivation as the other 100-plus species in the genus. The rosette can reach 5 inches across.

Echeveria nodulosa: The striking coloration on this *Echeveria* appears to have been applied by a painter. The line that runs along the middle of the leaf is deep maroon in color, as are the other leaf markings. Native to southern Mexico, *E. nodulosa* often grows as an epiphyte, that is, it lives on the branches of trees. It is slow growing and does best with frequent misting rather than a drenching in water. Orchid growers will recognize this

Echeveria nodulosa

trait among epiphytic plants in general. As such, it requires a slightly different treatment than that outlined for other species in this genus. As a houseplant, grow it in a container of freely draining mix with only a small amount of organic matter, and water only when the potting mix is dry. Mist regularly and feed a weak solution of fertilizer (one-fourth the strength recommended on the package) about every month or six weeks during the spring and summer. Eventually, the plant forms multiple stems and becomes a striking specimen.

Echeveria runyonii 'Topsy Turvy': The reversed grooves on the leaves give this cultivar its name. Prized for the sculptural effect it brings to arrange-ments, this selection of a Mexican species from the Chihuahuan Desert is both widely available and easy to grow. In good light, many specimens develop red-tinged leaf margins. Considered a "medium-sized" echeveria by growers, it reaches 8 inches in diameter.

Echeveria setosa: Also known as "Mexican firecracker," this species may be distinguished from other echeverias by its fuzzy, lime-green leaves. The plant will eventually grow into a treelike form if thoughtfully pruned. Normally, all echeverias will lose leaves from the root end of the stem. Plants absorb the stored water and nutrients from these leaves, which then shrivel and turn brown, eventu-

From left: Echeveria runyonii *'Topsy Turvy'*, Echeveria setosa; *opposite:* Echeveria lilacina

Clockwise from top left: Sedum acre *'Gold Moss'*, Sedum dasyphyllum, Sedum grisebachii, Sedum makinoi

ally leaving the rosette perched atop an elongated "trunk." Severing the rosette with a little piece of the stem attached won't hurt a thing. Pop the severed top into a pot with the stem stuck in the potting mix, and it will make roots and continue to grow. Keep tending the root portion as if nothing had happened, and it will produce several small rosettes from the cut end. Allow these to grow, and they will separately form new, elongated stems. Within a couple of growing seasons, the plant will come to resemble a small tree. When plants are happy, they will produce multiple, long-lasting bloom spikes of bright yellow and red-orange star-shaped flowers, the source of the "firecracker" moniker. You can also apply this pruning technique successfully to other echeveria varieties, as previously mentioned.

SEDUM

Widespread across Europe, Asia, and the Middle East, sedums comprise some 200 species, according to the most recent botanical evaluation. Most are winter hardy in the temperate zone, and indeed many are from extreme alpine habitats, but only a few are regularly cultivated as houseplants. (Recent research has resulted in the splitting of the genus into multiple genera. Nevertheless, nurseries and garden centers retain the old usage of the name.) In general, sedums are low, creeping plants with small, succulent leaves and stems that root into the soil as they grow. Some are so adaptable they are considered invasive pests where they have become established members of the flora. The name is derived

from the Latin *sedeo*, "to sit," in reference to the plant's habit of "sitting" on rocks.

Sedum acre 'Gold Moss': A cultivar of a common European species, the tiny, golden-yellow leaves of this sedum work well as a ground cover in containers and terrariums. Like all the members of this group, it benefits from a cool to cold rest in winter, with minimal water. Adventitious roots are readily produced, making it easy to propagate.

Sedum dasyphyllum: This attractive European species grows equally easily outdoors or as a houseplant. Also known as Corsican stonecrop, it works well as a ground cover in container gardens, terrariums, and other group arrangements. Try pairing it with *S. acre* 'Gold Moss' for a great color combination. The steel blue of *S. dasyphyllum* contrasts perfectly with the lemon-yellow *S. acre*.

Sedum grisebachii: Tight clusters of tiny leaves with a translucent bump at the tip of each leaf characterize this stonecrop. Often grown outdoors as a ground cover, it will also thrive as a houseplant if given a cool, dry winter rest.

Sedum makinoi: Known variously as "Japanese golden sedum" or "elephant bush" in the nursery trade, this serviceable sedum from Japan is an ideal choice for mixed plantings or an individual container. The flattened leaves, each about half the size of a dime, grow from a dark, reddish-brown stem. The contrast is appealing and is heightened in the cultivar 'Ogon' with golden-yellow leaves. In summer, the plants are covered with yellow, star-shaped flowers. As with other sedums, it is easily started from stem cuttings, no doubt enhancing its popularity with hobbyists and nurseries alike.

Sedum morganianum: "Burro's tail" is the common name for this member of the *Sedum* genus. The plant has a trailing stem about a ¼ inch in diameter from which elongated, swollen leaves emerge densely, making the entire branch look like a 2-inch-thick, pale blue-green rope. Display these plants in hanging baskets to maximize the impact of their pendant growth habit. Any growing mix for succulents will suit them. Water when the medium is dry to a depth of 1 inch, and feed regularly during the growing season to produce the largest specimens. Individual leaves are easily rooted to produce additional specimens. A cultivar with especially fat, rounded leaves is *S. morganianum* 'Burrito.'

Sedum nussbaumerianum: This large-leaved sedum looks great in mixed container plantings. The cultivar 'Coppertone' has striking red-brown metallic coloration that pairs extremely well with the blue to blue-gray tones of many other succulents. It has no special growing requirements.

Sedum sieboldii: Lovely fragrant pink blooms in late summer are the reward for growing this winter-hardy species. It adapts well to containers indoors but must be given a period of cold dormancy in winter in order to bloom again. Sometimes called "October daphne," this and other fall-blooming sedums have recently been reclassified by botanists. Numerous cultivated varieties have been developed by growers. This group of plants generally prefers shade, but some of the cultivated ones can take full sun without burning. General cultivation requirements are the same as for others in this group.

SEMPERVIVUM

Sempervivum cultivars: Native to North Africa, Europe, and the Near East, sempervivums have won the hearts of succulent growers for centuries. Also known as "hen and chicks" because the main plant bears numerous plantlets on short stems, they are also sometimes called "houseleeks" in reference to their presumed ability to ward off harm if grown on a thatched roof. Any of the many varieties will eventually cover the surface of a pot with offspring, or the chicks can be separated and potted individually to produce new plants. Plants do best with a period of dry cold in winter. Although commonly used in outdoor landscapes, they can be grown as houseplants if the cold winter rest can be arranged.

Clockwise from top left: Sedum sieboldii, Sedum morganianum, Sedum nussbaumerianum, Sempervivum *'Oddity'*

Clockwise from top left: Senecio radicans, Ceropegia sandersonii, Ceropegia woodii, Hoya *species*

Vines

A small number of desirable succulents have a vining habit. These plants are best displayed either in a hanging basket, a large pot with a trellis, or in a pot set on a high shelf to permit the trailing stems to be observed to best effect. A surprising number of vine succulents are in the milkweed family.

Ceropegia sandersonii: Known as "parachute flower," *C. sandersonii* is a tough, slow-growing vine with thick green stems and occasional heart-shaped green leaves. Out of bloom it is unremarkable, but the flowers, which can be produced in abundance for weeks at a time, are fascinatingly complex. Parachute flower can be allowed to grow with reckless abandon during the warmer months, and then it can be cut back hard and given a winter rest in cooler, drier, and shadier conditions. Bring it out again the following spring, feed and water every two weeks, and it will respond with its unique floral display until shortening days and cooling temperatures signal the time for another rest period.

Ceropegia woodii: "String of hearts," or "rosary vine," is another South African succulent vine. While it produces an unusual pinkish-purple flower, the plant is most often grown for the perfectly heart-shaped, variegated foliage on long, trailing stems. The leaves are thick and flat and could be mistaken for plastic at first glance. The plant grows slowly but with time will develop into an impressive specimen. Culture is as described for *C. sandersonii*. The winter rest is essential.

Hoya species: Known as "wax plant," *Hoya* vines have been popular houseplants for decades. They prefer more soil moisture during the growing season than most succulents but demand much drier conditions in winter. Feeding every two weeks, beginning with the onset of spring, will help promote the waxy, white, richly fragrant blooms in summer. To keep the plants in bounds, prune lightly before the winter dormant period, but do not remove old flower stalks, as they will give rise to new blooms the following season. Plants resent being repotted. Therefore, use a mostly inert potting medium with no more than 10 percent organic matter and select a pot that will easily accommodate the root ball for more than one season. Two species are commonly available. *Hoya carnosa* is larger and more luxurious in its growth form than *H. lanceolata*. The genus is native to eastern Asia and Australia, with over 100 species. Nevertheless, only the two most common ones are widely available. The others are collector's items. Note that the foliage of all hoyas is toxic.

Senecio radicans: Known commonly as "fishhook plant," this vining succulent is a member of the vast aster family. It is easily maintained and somewhat slow growing. The blue-green stems bear short, fat,

Senecio rowleyanus

Living Stones and Their Relatives

This group of succulents, found mostly in South Africa, lives underground, with only the uppermost portion of the stem exposed. Typically, the above-ground portion features a translucent window, permitting sunlight to reach the photosynthetic cells protected deep inside the stem. Several genera of these plants have adapted themselves to growth in extremely arid conditions where they are camouflaged as pebbles lying among countless others in dry swales. Widely available, the plants can be tricky in cultivation. Some successful growers place them in pure sand, and water only occasionally.

cylindrical leaves that are recurved at their pointed tips like fishhooks. Given bright, indirect light and a well-drained growing medium, it will slowly grow into an impressive specimen. This is among the more commonly available trailing succulents.

Senecio rowleyanus: Commonly known as "string of pearls," this slow-growing plant eventually develops into a spectacular display. Best grown in a hanging basket to display the characteristic bead-like leaves, the plant is naturally found in a limited area of the Eastern Cape province of South Africa. Cultivation for many years, however, has brought it within reach of gardeners everywhere. Each of the round leaves has a slit-like window. Under good conditions, plants produce small, cinnamon-scented flowers.

Fenestraria rhopalophylla ssp. *aurantiaca:* "Baby toes" is the cute common name given to this South African species. The subspecies *aurantiaca* has yellow flowers that look like asters. This plant is frequently found growing in pure sand and derives the moisture it requires for survival from fog that arrives daily from the nearby sea. When grown as a house-plant, it benefits from regular misting, or a very light watering about every two weeks. The individual stems are topped with a translucent "window" that allows sunlight into the photosynthetic cells on the interior. Much of the rest of the plant lies buried in the sand. It needs a bone-dry rest period in the winter months.

Lithops species: *Lithops* species surely rank as some of the hardiest succulents, at least in their natural

Clockwise from top left: Lithops *stem structure,* Fenestraria aurantiaca *Baby Toes,* Fenestraria aurantiaca *flower*

habitat. Known collectively as "living stones," the several dozen species are found in South Africa and Namibia in what appear to be some of the harshest desert conditions imaginable. Blistering summers, cold winters, and no rainfall for years at a stretch characterize the inhospitable climate of the regions preferred by these plants. This observation might suggest that they are a cinch in cultivation, but that is not always the case. Too often, plants are killed by their keepers out of a lack of understanding of the natural growth cycle. Each individual consists of two leaves that are mostly buried. The top eighth of an inch or so is above the soil line, and is mostly occupied by the translucent window. Different patterns of color on the window contribute to the plant's camouflage among surrounding pebbles and stones. The two leaves may be almost completely fused together with a narrow gap between, or they may be more widely separated, giving the plant a two-lobed appearance. In both types, the flowers are produced from the gap.

The blooms are daisylike, in yellow or white. A group of plants in a single pot can produce quite a display. After flowering, the pair of leaves splits apart and a new pair appears, typically perpendicular to the old pair. Hobbyists must take care to give the plant no water at all from this point until the new growth is fully developed and the old leaves are shriveled and brown. Adding water during this process will cause the old leaves to swell and choke off the new growth, resulting in the death of the plant. In addition to these peculiarities, living stones need the brightest light you can provide and an atmosphere of low humidity. With proper attention to their needs, *Lithops* will slowly form a cluster, and the floral display will get better with each passing year.

Other living stones: Several additional genera, including *Argyroderma*, *Conophytum*, *Dinteranthus*, *Lapidaria*, *Pleiospilos*, produce "living stone" growth forms. Many of them also have brilliant, colorful flowers. Growers interested in giving these intriguing plants a try should seek out specimens online or from specialty nurseries. Some are demanding in cultivation, others relatively easy.

Succulents Worth Seeking

Here I have chosen to lump together a variety of succulent species that are less commonly seen in the nursery trade, but by no means are any of them rarities. Although individual species may deviate somewhat from the standard pattern of care described for most of the plants in this book, these plants can generally be successfully maintained in bright light with a growing medium that is free-draining with 25 percent to 45 percent organic matter. Most benefit from a cooler, drier rest period during the winter months and bright light, with regular fertilization, during the growing season.

Adenium obesum **and relatives:** Adeniums have been reasonably common in the nursery trade for about 25 years, and recently the popularity of succulents in general has caused them to appear even in supermarket floral departments. Known as "desert rose" plants, *Adenium* species and hybrids are valued for the showy, often fragrant bloom displays that last for weeks at a time. The leaves grow from the tops of the swollen caudex, which is covered with smooth, gray, leathery bark. The most widely grown species, *A. obsesum*, produces hot pink blooms in clusters. Unlike many other succulents, adeniums respond well to weekly watering, or even more, during hot weather. They will not, however, tolerate winter moisture and should be kept bone dry for four months. The onset of the dormant period will be signified by leaves turning yellow and dropping. Cease watering at this point and keep the plants dry until the end of the dormancy period, whereupon the appearance of new leaves signals the onset of another season of growth and the renewed need for water and food. Well-drained soil is essential, as is warmth. Cool, cloudy, and damp conditions can spell disaster. Some cultivars may not drop leaves on their own. If they look lush into October,

Adenium obesum

Adromischus cristatus

stop watering to force them into dormancy, and keep them dry until the end of January.

Adromischus cristatus: The "Key lime pie plant" gets its name from the unusual triangular leaves, their outer edges typically scalloped like the edge of a pie crust. From South Africa, this and other members of the genus provide some truly bizarre forms. The leaves can be beautifully patterned with UV-shielding pigments, and the range of leaf shapes includes spiny globes shaped like the fruits of a sweetgum tree. Some have leaves shaped like bowling pins, while others resemble sore-throat lozenges. Any of these plants is worth growing. *Adromischus cristatus* produces adventitious roots along the stem, and the lower leaves shrivel and drop with regularity. Eventually the stem bears a coat of brown roots. The shaggy roots surrounding the stem help to trap fog that often sweeps across the plants' natural habitat. These plants remain small in size and thus are good houseplant choices. Some of the less common species do best if kept on the dry side in summer, although *A. cristatus* and its several forms will tolerate summer moisture. Bright light and a cold, dry winter rest will be rewarded by good spring and summer growth, culminating in the production of small, white, star-shaped flowers on long, arching stems late in the season. Cultivated forms of *A. cristatus* may lack the scalloped edge or may be yellow-green in color, or both.

Aeonium species: From the Canary Islands, with some species ranging as far as East Africa, comes this genus of succulents closely related to *Sempervivum*. About 30 species share a growth habit consisting of upright branches topped with rosettes of leaves. Like the similar *Echeveria* species, *Aeonium* is often grown for the leaf rosettes alone and not allowed to develop the typical shrub-like form. Among the most popular cultivars is *A. arboreum* 'Zwartkop,' which has leaves that are so dark purple as to appear black. Individual rosettes die after producing a bloom spike of yellow flowers. Additional rosettes are abundantly produced, however, and plants can be grown into impressive specimens. As a general rule, the rosettes close more or less tightly during the dry, dormant period. Grow *Aeonium* in any mix suitable for other succulents and give a dry, cool rest period.

Aloe juvenna: "Tiger tooth aloe," as this species is commonly known, is a native of Kenya. Having become quite popular in cultivation, it nevertheless is more difficult to propagate than some other succulents. It will not root from leaf cuttings but does form offsets that can eventually be separated from the main plant. This is best done when it is time to repot. If the roots are hopelessly entangled, cut the plants apart with a pair of sterilized pruners or florist's scis-

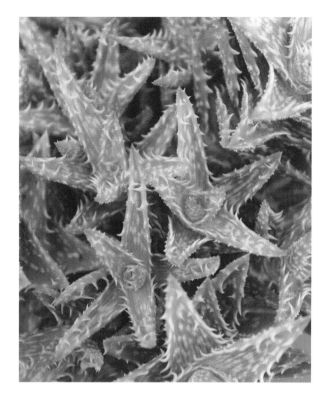

Aloe juvenna

sors. Make sure each piece has some roots, and repot in fresh potting mix. Water well, then place the plants where they will receive indirect light for a week or so before moving them into full sun. This plant is adaptable and easy to grow, a great choice for the beginning succulent enthusiast. Owing perhaps to the difficulty in propagation, it is not as common in the nursery trade as its ease of culture might indicate.

Aloe 'Pink Blush': Hybrid aloes do not require any special care, and many are even more adaptable as houseplants than the species from which they are

derived. *Aloe* 'Pink Blush' is no exception, with its variegated seafoam green leaves with pink edging. The pink flowers are also attractive. Many hybrid aloes remain small, having been derived from naturally diminutive species.

Crassula sarcocaulis, Crassula tetragona: Also known as the "bonsai jade plant," this little treelike crassula is native to eastern South Africa, like the more familiar *C. ovata*. Along with *C. tetragona*, the "pine tree bonsai," it is hugely popular for creating bonsai displays. Both adapt easily to container cultivation, regular pruning, and a general lack of attention. Water these plants about once a month, depending upon the potting mix and container type, and feed annually at the beginning of the growing season. These plants normally grow in winter but will adapt to the summer schedule of the Northern

Clockwise from left: Aloe *'Pink Bush'*, Crassula sarcocaulis, Crassula tetragona

Euphorbia horrida

Hemisphere. They are also among the most cold-hardy members of the genus and can be grown outdoors as far north as Georgia.

EUPHORBIA

There are more than a thousand species of *Euphorbia*, with about half of them considered to be succulents. Many are standards in the horticulture trade. Botanists have subjected this group to multiple taxonomic revisions, but most of the horticulturally important species fall into two groups: those with enlarged stems and no spines, and those with spines. Either group may have some members with leaves and some without. All euphorbias produce a milky sap. The sap may be irritating to sensitive skin, and some varieties produce extremely toxic sap. As a general rule, the popular ones are harmless, other than the sharp spines. These species are generally found in South Africa, with some ranging across the hemisphere to Asia. As with many other popular succulent varieties, euphorbias should receive infrequent watering during the growing season and little or none in winter. Provide bright light and temperatures in excess of 50°F. Plants will appreciate cooler temperatures during the dormant winter period. Grow euphorbias in commercial cactus potting mix. Feed plants monthly during the growing season, using a soluble fertilizer at half the manufacturer's recommended strength. Plants also respond well to timed-release fertilizer mixed in with the potting soil, again at half the manufacturer's recommendation.

Euphorbia horrida: Can you deduce from the scientific name that this plant has sharp spines, and lots of them? The spines are also venomous. Definitely not a choice for a household with small children or rambunctious pets, this species nevertheless has a certain charm, like a scary movie. It grows easily under care as described for the other euphorbias. It is also the most cold-tolerant member of the succulent euphorbia clan, surviving temperatures into the teens.

Euphorbia obesa: Sometimes called "bishop's hat," this euphorbia remains a compact little ball for most of its lifetime. At first glance, this spurge closely resembles a squat, rounded cactus. Rows of tiny spines radiating from the apex of the domelike stem call to mind the clerical headdress. Grow this species in a sharply drained mixture with less than 50 percent organic matter. Water it about every two weeks during the growing season and about every six weeks during its winter rest period. As they age, male plants become more like cylinders, while the females remain squat. Flowers are seldom produced outside of greenhouse conditions, but in all euphorbias the male and female flowers are borne on separate plants.

Euphorbia tirucalli: Leafless, thickened green stems that branch regularly characterize this unusual euphorbia. In the cultivar 'Fire Sticks,' the tips of the branches turn a vivid orange-red in bright light. You can break off a branch and root it in potting mix to

Euphorbia obesa

Left: Euphorbia tirucalli; *right: Bushy euphorbia*

produce another plant. Grow in any mix suitable for succulents and water once a week during the growing season. Give the plant a dry, cool, winter rest.

Bushy euphorbias: In cultivation, some *Euphorbia* species develop elongated, floppy, woody stems and take on the appearance of a small shrub. The accompanying photo is an example of an unknown species growing in a greenhouse at the University of Tennessee in Knoxville. Smaller specimens that look like jointed corals or a collection of green bones will eventually develop this appearance. Most likely, the growth pattern results from the relatively "lush" conditions to be found in cultivation, as opposed to the harsh demands of the plants' natural habitat.

Gasteria carinata v. verrucosa: Bright red leaf tips characterize this plant, which is native to the western cape of South Africa. Gasterias are such reliable horticultural subjects, they have lost favor with succulent specialists who consider them too easy to merit attention. However, for the houseplant enthusiast, they offer some small to medium plants that look great and tolerate a lot of neglect. They prefer shade, another characteristic that lends itself to indoor cultivation. A growing medium with some organic matter

Gasteria carinata v. verrucosa

recommended for other succulents. Its appearance reveals its close relationship to *Echeveria*, with which it is sometimes hybridized.

Graptopetalum pachyphyllum: Another Mexican species, this one is easy to grow and popular as a houseplant. Leaf cuttings root with little encouragement and soon will produce a large collection of plants. The leaves sometimes bear an orange tint in bright sunshine.

Haworthia fasciata: Arguably the most attractive of the commonly available *Haworthia*, this one can be distinguished from *H. attenuata* by the arrangement of the white tubercles on the leaves, which form distinct bands, giving it the common name "zebra plant." Reddish-brown pigment that forms in the leaves when the plants are grown in bright light also contributes to the attractiveness of this species. Grow it alongside *H. attenuata* in similar conditions.

Haworthia retusa: Another South African species, this beautiful plant occurs in multiple forms. Many cultivated varieties that are labeled as this species are actually hybrids involving the related *H. turgida*, but that hardly matters for purposes of horticulture. This subgroup of *Haworthia* is distinguished by the lack of offset formation that makes others easy to propagate. In addition, the flattened leaf tips are outfitted with windows that allow sunlight to reach the photosynthetic cells inside without exposing too much of the plant to predators. Often these windows

and biweekly watering suits this and other members of the genus. That is, they like more water than most of the plants mentioned in this book. Numerous hybrid forms are available, making exact identification somewhat difficult for a given specimen. However, in terms of care they are all so similar that the suggestions given should work for any of them.

Graptopetalum paraguayense: The "ghost plant," as this variety is known, is among the easiest of succulents to propagate. In fact, leaves can be dislodged with very little effort. Each one will grow roots and form a new plant within a short time. Besides the species, multiple cultivars and hybrids of this plant exist. All are easily grown with the same methods

Clockwise from top left: Graptopetalum paraguayense, Graptopetalum pachyphyllum, Haworthia retusa, Haworthia fasciata

Jovibarba hirta (Sempervivum hirta) *ssp.* arenaria

are marked with colors and patterns that make them resemble stained glass. The variation in leaf decoration has led to widespread misidentification of cultivated forms. Nevertheless, all are arguably worth growing. Best success will be had with a potting mix that contains very little organic matter. Mist plants frequently, or water about every 10 days. The natural range of this group is near the coast in the vicinity of Cape Town.

Jovibarba hirta (Sempervivum hirta) **ssp. arenaria:** A relative of hen and chicks, and sometimes included in the genus *Sempervivum*, these plants may also be called "rollers" due to their unique method of propagation. Unlike the other hen and chicks, the offsets are produced on tall stems. This adaptation allows the offsets to break off and fall or roll some distance from the parent plant before taking root. Native to the Alps, the plants take cold well, but not if their roots remain moist. They are adaptable to indoor cultivation, provided you give them a cool-to-cold and dry rest period in the winter.

KALANCHOE

Pronounced "kah-LAN-koh-ee," this is another group of horticulturally important succulents from the African continent. Most of the popular species are from Madagascar, but additional ones, some quite rare, occur in southeast Africa and eastward to India. The origins of the name are unknown, but may reside in an Indian dialect. The commonly grown plants in this group are found in areas with

Kalanchoe blossfeldiana

strong differentiation between wet and dry seasons. Many are thus more like typical houseplants than the succulents that come from arid zones. As a rule, all of the kalanchoes can be grown in commercial cactus potting mix, with regular watering and feeding during the growing season and a dry winter rest. Some species produce abundant miniature plantlets from the leaves. They are thus easy to reproduce as houseplants and can become an invasive pest in areas where they are able to overwinter.

CAUTION: Many kalanchoe plants are toxic to pets.

Kalanchoe beharensis: Tough, leathery, blue-green leaves with brown fuzz on their upper surfaces characterize the "felt plant." Although it is capable of growing to treelike dimensions, this plant will dwarf if maintained in a relatively small container. The leaves, however, will retain their normal size, even though the branches remain short. This can be interesting or ugly, depending upon your preferences. Care is as for other succulents, infrequent watering and a cool, dry winter rest.

Kalanchoe blossfeldiana: This species is so ubiquitous in the nursery trade that it is sometimes referred to as the "grocery store kalanchoe," and not always with complimentary intent. The flowers, easily forced in a greenhouse, come in bright, primary colors and pastel shades. You may see them on the shelves of florist shops and in the floral section of the grocery store at almost any time of year.

From top: Kalanchoe beharensis, Kalanchoe thyrsiflora

The glossy, deep green foliage sets off the upright flower cluster perfectly. They have been grown as gift plants for decades, and many people simply toss them in the trash after the flowers fade. However, prompt removal of the spent flower stalks, along with regular fertilization and good light, will promote re-blooming. Nevertheless, plants can sometimes refuse to bloom again on the windowsill. The remedy is to start new plants from leaf cuttings (see page 58). As these mature, they will bloom. In Madagascar, where the plant originated, bloom time is spring, but in the Northern Hemisphere plants will bloom during the traditional holiday season. Greenhouse specimens can be forced into bloom as the nursery desires by controlling the length of the daylight period.

Kalanchoe thyrsiflora: "Flapjack plant," as this species is known commonly, produces big, rounded, flat leaves in a rosette arrangement. Mature plants will produce a tall inflorescence covered with a dusty, white powder and multiple tiny blooms. If this bloom spike is allowed to form seeds, the plant may die. Instead, cut off the flower spike near its base after the uppermost blooms have opened. The plant should respond by producing a second rosette of leaves adjacent to the old one. Keep doing this, and you will have a cluster of smaller flapjacks growing from a common base. New plants can also be started from individual leaves, but this should be done prior to the formation of the bloom spike, typically in late summer. In good light, individual leaves are rimmed in red.

Collector's Items

Among this group are species that seldom appear in the nursery trade outside of specialty growers. Diligent hobbyists who want to add these species to their collection should search online for sources. Sometimes your local garden center may be willing to locate a specimen for you, but you should expect to pay a premium for this service.

Agave parryi v. couesii: Remaining compact enough to be grown as a houseplant, this is the most commonly encountered of the smaller mem-

Agave parryi v. couesii

From left: Pereskia aculeata *foliage,* Pereskia aculeata *aureoles,* Pereskiopsis aquosa

bers of the *Agave* genus. Capable of reaching 4 feet in diameter, it is more often much smaller. The leaves are gray-blue and not as spiny as in some agaves. The variety *couesii*, pictured here, is found in central Arizona. Preferring limestone soils in nature, it grows in standard mixes in cultivation.

Pereskia aculeata: At first glance, you would think *Pereskia* is a tree, based on the woody, branching stem and glossy leaves. But a closer look at the stem reveals aureoles and spines, placing it in the cactus family. Native to tropical America, it is worth seeking out for its striking waxy-petaled white flowers with yellow centers. Known as Barbados gooseberry, the plant produces edible fruits. It is easily grown into a small, flowering tree. Despite the edibility of the fruit and leaves, *Pereskia* is considered an invasive pest in localities, such as South Africa, where it has been introduced. Plants should not be imported into areas of the United States where it is capable of over-wintering, including the Deep South and Southwest. For hobbyists in cooler climates, it makes a great houseplant.

Pereskiopsis aquosa: Related to *Pereskia*, this plant is another cactus that does not look like a cactus. It is much less common in cultivation than *Pereskia* and is not as easily grown. In cooler climates, be extremely careful of overwatering when the plant is not in active growth, usually during the winter months. Too much water at this time will lead to rotting of the stem. It is sought out because of its compact size and the glossy, dark green leaves.

Stapelia gigantea **and relatives:** These durable plants bear a bloom that smells like rotting meat to attract the flies that pollinate them. Once classified among the milkweeds, the group is now assigned to the oleander family. Of more interest to houseplant enthusiasts are the remarkable flowers, which look like enormous starfish. The succulent stems in cross section look like crosses, their incurved sides forming four edges decorated with scallops. Native to East Africa as far north as Tanzania, the plants respond well to bright light, limited watering, and weak fertilization monthly during the growing season. Related genera *Huernia* and *Caralluma* are similar and produce flowers in a range of bold coloration. *Stapelia flavopurpurea* bears flowers that look remarkably like a common starfish. Any of these botanical curiosities is worth seeking out for a serious collection.

Stapelia gigantea

135

CACTI

Popular Groups of Cacti

The cactus family is largely confined to North and South America, with only a few Old World species. For our purposes in this section, the group comprises spinous plants that frequently produce showy flowers. Larger individuals thrive in sun and heat, while dwarf plants are often adapted to live in the shade of something larger. All benefit from a cool, dry, and cloudy rest period in the winter months. They are also more sensitive than other succulents to improper watering. Plants can rot from the roots up without giving an outward indication until it is too late. Grow them in media with no more than 40 percent to 45 percent organic matter. Limit watering to about once a week in summer. Plants moved outdoors may need protection from excessive rainfall, depending upon local weather. Feed sparingly at the beginning of the growing season and at three- to six-week intervals thereafter; do not feed at all in winter. The reward for your careful efforts is the appearance of flowers, typically produced from early spring throughout summer, depending upon the species. Some atypical cacti are found in rainforest habitats and are also popular in cultivation. We will discuss them separately later in this chapter.

Cephalocereus senilis: Known as the "old man cactus," this one is grown for its shaggy appearance, the result of long, silvery hairs that cover younger plants. Eventually, the plant will reach a height of about a foot and will produce a cluster of unbranched stems. Flowers may be white, red, or yellow but are seldom seen on cultivated specimens. Individuals do not flower until they are 20 years old or so. Like other cacti, feed the plant monthly during the growing season, water when the soil is dry to a depth of 1 inch, and do not feed or water during the winter dormant period. If your goal is to obtain a mature cluster that may possibly bloom, repot every spring and pay attention to feeding on a regular schedule.

Cleistocactus winteri

Cleistocactus winteri: A trailing species, the "golden rat tail cactus" lives up to its common name. It grows fairly rapidly for a cactus and is best displayed in a hanging basket. The bright orange or salmon-colored flowers are produced abundantly and last several days. Plants bloom from spring to summer. A well-grown specimen can have stems over 3 feet in length and dozens of blooms. Because of its fast growth rate, this cactus should be fed once a month during spring and summer when it is in active growth. Cease feeding and reduce watering during the winter months. It is native to Bolivia.

Echinocactus grusonii: The "golden barrel cactus" slowly grows to enormous size. It bears sharp spines that can inflict a painful puncture. Nevertheless, it is a durable and reliable plant that retains considerable popularity among cactus fans. It requires nothing special in the way of growing conditions, thrives in summer sun, and needs a bright, cool, dry rest during the winter months. This is another species that does not bloom until it achieves considerable size, and in any case the blooms are not as spectacular as those on some other cacti.

Echinopsis species: Some 128 cacti comprise this genus from South America. Commonly called "hedgehog cacti," they range in size from treelike giants to compact, globose forms that are popular in cultivation. Among the various common names applied to the group, "Easter lily cactus" perhaps best describes the large, showy, often fragrant

From top: Cephalocereus senilis, Echinocactus grusonii

flowers produced near the tips of the stems. The flowers open at night and have faded and wilted by the following afternoon. Plants may, however, produce multiple blooms over a period of several days. Large, well-grown specimens may have many blooms open simultaneously. They are easily grown

Echinopsis *species*

and should have a dry, cool rest in winter to promote spring blooms. Many varieties readily produce offsets, and these will bloom the second spring after separating them from the parent. Feed at the beginning of the growing season and then monthly thereafter until autumn.

Notocactus species: Included here because of recent name changes, this genus name may appear on the nursery tag of any of several species of cacti that you may encounter. All are now classified in the genus *Parodia*, discussed later in this section.

Opuntia species: Prickly pears are native to the southwestern and southern United States, as well as Mexico and Central America. They have been introduced in other locations. Many bear edible fruits. Smaller species are suitable for a windowsill collection, while larger ones require a big pot and plenty of room. The latter are best left as outdoor subjects in areas where they are winter hardy, which includes large portions of the United States. Spectacular flowers 3 or 4 inches in diameter are produced in midsummer, followed by wine-red fruits. The fruits are edible and used to make jelly. Young, tender "paddles" from certain varieties of this cactus are scraped free of their spines and sliced into strips to make a vegetable dish known as *nopalitos*. The flavor is reminiscent of green beans. The "bunny ear cactus," *O. microdasys*, lacks spines and instead has white glochidia growing from each aureole. Found in central Mexico, it is also sometimes known as "polka dot cactus." The closely related and more northerly distributed, *O. rufida* looks almost identical, but the glochidia are rusty brown. Both species are popular in cultivation because they remain smaller than most others of the genus and because of the droll appearance resembling a cartoon rabbit with upright ears. Beware, however, of the glochidia, as they embed themselves in the skin at the slight-

Clockwise from top left: Opuntia *fruits*, Opuntia microdasys, Pachycereus pringlei, Opuntia rufida

Parodia *species*

est touch and are both irritating and difficult to remove. Try pulling them out by placing the sticky side of a piece of adhesive or duct tape over the glochidia.

NOTE: This genus has recently been split into several genera. *Opuntia* continues to be the name used in the nursery trade.

Pachycereus pringlei: The false saguaro cactus grows into a beautifully sculptural houseplant. (The true saguaro, a protected species that grows to the height of a small tree, is unsuitable for cultivation in any but the largest conservatory.) *Pachycereus* is a great choice for a large pot. Placed in a sunny corner, it will slowly develop into an impressive specimen. When mature, it produces an impressive floral display.

Parodia species: A genus of characteristically ribbed cacti from South America, the various species remain relatively small and are popular with hobbyists. The terminal flowers are often strikingly colored. Sensitive to overwatering, *Parodia* plants must also be protected from cold. They are truly tropical and resent temperatures below 50°F. Basic care is as outlined for all cacti.

MAMMILLARIA

This genus of Mexican cacti is hugely popular because most of the species remain small, they are easily grown from seeds, and they flower readily on a windowsill. All will benefit from a summer outdoors in dappled sunshine, but they can remain indoors indefinitely, if need be. The common name for members of this group, "pincushion cactus," reflects the typical plump, round form found among the species. Some are more columnar, and a few are egg shaped. Flowers are typically daisylike, but some do not follow this pattern, at least not obviously. Flower color and size may determine the popularity of a particular cultivar. Some produce tiny white flowers, while in other species the brightly colored flowers may seem too large for the plant bearing them. All species should be given a dry, cool rest during winter. Flowers appear from spring through summer, depending upon the species. Grow any of them in commercial cactus pot-

ting mix and feed monthly during the growing season. To encourage plants to reach flowering size, repot them every year until they are mature. Then repot every two to three years. Allow soil to dry to a depth of 1 inch during the growing season. In winter, water even less frequently, perhaps once every six weeks, depending upon the retentiveness of the growing medium. Cooler, shadier conditions for the winter rest help encourage flowering the following season. These plants are excellent choices for beginners interested in the cactus clan.

Mammillaria elegans: No, those are not red chili peppers protruding from the side of the *Mammillaria* plant in the accompanying photograph. Those are the fruits. Eventually, they will dry up, turn brown, and sag downward, spilling out the tiny seeds. Enterprising hobbyists can collect the seeds before they are released and use them to produce numerous additional plants. Fresh seed is best, although older seed will eventually germinate, too. No special treatment is required to entice this easy species to bloom in pink shades.

Mammillaria elongata: The yellow coloration of the stems of this *Mammillaria* offers an appealing change from the greens and blue-greens of its cousins. Native to central Mexico, it produces a ring of small yellowish flowers around each stem tip.

Mammillaria gracilis: Known as "thimble cactus," this easy-to-grow species blooms readily. It produces

Mammillaria haageana

white flowers about ¼ inch in diameter in late winter. Plants bloom for about a month. Care is the same as for other mammillarias.

Mammillaria haageana: This one is another easy-to-grow species from Mexico. It is widespread in cultivation and readily produces its small, pink flowers in a circle around the apex of the stem in early spring. As plants mature, they begin producing branches and offsets, and the bloom display gets better and better as a result. Feed regularly during the growing season, as described for other species, and give plants a cool, dry winter rest period. Repot mature plants every two to three years. The best time to repot is after the blooms have faded.

Clockwise from top left: Mammillaria elegans, Mammillaria elongata, Mammillaria gracilis

Atypical Cacti

Some members of the cactus family live as epiphytes. That is, they grow upon the branches of trees, with their roots exposed. In this, they are more like orchids than they are like other cacti. While none of them are especially beautiful when out of bloom, the floral display can be stunning, and this is the reason for growing them.

Disocactus flagelliformis: The huge, strikingly red flowers of this cactus are produced in spring and appear most often on plants that are somewhat root-bound. Therefore, keep the plant in the same pot for as long as possible. Use a freely draining growing mix with added sand or gravel. The plants are ideal subjects for display in a hanging basket. Keep them in bright, indirect light and water when the soil is dried out during the growing season. From spring through summer, apply a balanced, soluble fertilizer at half the manufacturer's recommended strength. Cease feeding as fall arrives, cut back on water, and place the plant in a cool, shady location for a winter rest. Bring the plants back out into good light when new growth appears in early spring, and begin watering. Blooms should appear within a few weeks.

Epiphyllum cultivars: Often called "orchid cactus" because of its similar growth habit, 19 species of this genus are found in Central America. The

Disocactus flagelliformis

leaves are generally flattened, elongated, and scalloped on the edges, and the plants can slowly grow to an unwieldy size even in a small pot. Stems reach 18 to 30 inches in length, depending upon the variety. The blooms are large, showy, and range in color from white to red. In *E. oxypetalum*, among the most commonly grown species, the flowers are white, richly fragrant, and survive only one night. They open after dark, the process taking place so quickly the movement of the flower is readily apparent. Soon the fragrance becomes noticeable. By morning, the flowers have faded. New buds will repeat the show over

Epiphyllum oxypetalum

the next several days. Another popular species, *E. anguliger*, is known as "zigzag cactus" in the nursery trade. It produces fragrant, pale yellow flowers in autumn. In order to obtain blooms, the plants require a cool winter rest at temperatures below 60°F, but never colder than 35°F. Growth occurs mostly in spring and fall. Beginning in February, feed a low-nitrogen fertilizer about every two weeks until flower buds appear. Then, cease feeding altogether until October. Feed a balanced fertilizer monthly from October through December, but don't bother feeding in January

Clockwise from top left: Epiphyllum *cultivars*, Selenicereus anthonyanus *flower*, Epiphyllum anguliger, Hatiora rosea

Schlumbergera *cultivars*

and early February, when low light levels will cause growth to cease altogether. Besides the various species, hybrids among species and with closely related genera are available in the nursery trade, generally bringing a wider array of floral display to the *Epiphyllum* clan.

Selenicereus anthonyanus: This night-blooming epiphytic cactus has been around for a long time. Sometimes called "ric rac cactus," it goes by the name "night-blooming *Cereus*" among older gardeners. Like the blooms of the *Epiphyllum* species, the large, fragrant flowers of this cactus open at night. The opening happens quickly, in a few seconds. Uninitiated viewers may be quite surprised to see such rapid movement from a plant. Although it is easy to grow and the floral display can be truly spectacular, *Selenicereus* is too large to be accommodated by many people. Individual leaves easily reach 3 feet in length. If you have room to display it, a hanging basket works best. Plants should receive indirect sunshine, frequent misting, and regular fertilization during the growing season. After flowering, which typically occurs in late summer or autumn, the plants should have a dry, cool rest for about 90 days. The appearance of new growth is a signal to begin feeding and regular watering once again.

Hatiora species: Commonly called "Easter cactus," plants often appear in garden centers heavy with buds of the brilliant scarlet flowers a week or two before the Christian holiday. Too often, when the season has passed the plants fail to thrive and do not bloom again. Most often, the issue is watering—these plants are considerably fussier than some of their relatives. Neither too much nor too little water is tolerated. The "Goldilocks" zone for them seems to be a growing medium that remains barely moist at all times but is never soggy or allowed to dry out completely. Plants must have a cool period from November to January, with temperatures in the range of 45°F to 55°F. During the rest of the year, the daytime temperature should average 77°F.

During the growing season, feed a half-strength balanced fertilizer twice monthly. The plants grow best in indirect light and must be given shade if moved outdoors for the summer. Loss of leaf segments is a sure sign they are unhappy with the watering schedule.

Schlumbergera cultivars: Native to Brazil, the several species of *Schlumbergera* are commonly known as "Thanksgiving cactus," or "Christmas cactus." All are epiphytes or lithophytes (living on rocks) that do best in light shade and a humid atmosphere. Two groups are distinguished within the genus. The Truncata group has stem segments with pointed lobes, and the flowers are either horizontal or almost erect. Flowering occurs earlier in the season, and most of these plants will be identified as "Thanksgiving cactus." The Buckleyi group has rounded lobes on the stem segments, and the flowers generally are pendant, that is, they hang down below the level of the foliage. These plants bloom later than their cousins and are usually ascribed to the "Christmas cactus" genre. Thanksgiving cactus bears flowers that are asymmetrical or "zygomorphic," while the flowers of Christmas cactus are symmetrical. While both types of *Schlumbergera* are forgiving in cultivation, obtaining flowers requires careful attention to both the growing temperature and the day length. Like *Hatiora*, previously described, a constantly moist but never wet or dry growing medium is crucial to good culture. Happily, standard commercial potting mixes with peat and perlite work just fine. Overexposure to the sun, while not a problem indoors as a rule, can damage plants that are summered outdoors. Red pigmentation in the leaves is a sure sign of overly bright conditions. Plants should receive light, regular fertilization during the growing season from March to September. Reduce feeding as the bloom season approaches. A period of eight days at a temperature around 60°F and 12 to 16 hours of darkness per day has been shown to induce flower bud formation. Lack of attention to the lighting and temperature requirements of the plants to produce flowers no doubt has led to much frustration among novice growers.

ORCHIDS

I conclude our catalog of succulents for the windowsill with mention of a few members of the vast orchid clan. Many tropical orchids grow as epiphytes on the branches of trees, or even on rocks, where their roots are exposed and dry out quickly after a rain. Many of them have developed succulent "pseudobulbs," a portion of the stem that stores water. Like the other succulents included in this catalog, orchids must be grown in a well-aerated, fast-draining medium. They differ in their requirement for frequent light doses of fertilizer and a humid atmosphere.

Brassavola nodosa: Known as the "lady of the night," this orchid is the national flower of Costa Rica. Instead of pseudobulbs, it produces succulent leaves. It grows easily in a sunny window, potted in pure sphagnum moss. Water when the moss is dry and feed two or three times a month with a half-strength solution of soluble orchid fertilizer. Give the plant as much sun as possible and it will reward you with abundant scapes of white flowers that are richly fragrant at night. Plants grown on a windowsill and summered outdoors typically bloom in autumn. Greenhouse-grown plants can be almost ever-blooming. Repot the plants every three years.

Oncidium 'Sharry Baby': Who could resist blooms that smell like chocolate frosting? 'Sharry Baby' is one of the most popular hybrids in a popular genus of orchids. Deep maroon and cream-colored flowers are borne abundantly on long, arching stems. The floral display gets better and better each year as the plants grow larger. Pot in sphagnum moss and water when the moss is almost dry. Place in bright sun—an east or south window is ideal—and if possible display in a humid location. Feed with half-strength soluble orchid fertilizer at every watering, except once a month, when you should use plain water to flush out any accumulated salts.

Zygopetalum species: The orchids in this South American genus produce tall spikes of fragrant flowers, often in shades of blue or purple mixed with white. Besides several species, numerous hybrids are available. They are particularly intolerant of overly moist growing medium, and do best in hanging baskets or shallow pots (sometimes called "pans" in the horticulture trade). Pure fir bark, available at many garden centers and from some big-box stores, is the best growing medium. Choose a grade with pieces from ½ inch to 1 inch in diameter. Repot plants annually as new growth begins in spring. The plants are somewhat fragile, and care should be taken when repotting. Adding a teaspoon of dolomitic limestone to the potting medium is said to improve the toughness of the leaves and pseudobulbs.

Clockwise from top left: Oncidium *'Sharry Baby'*, Zygopetalum, Brassavola nodosa

ACKNOWLEDGMENTS

No book is ever truly the work of only the author. I have had lots of help along the way. Special thanks to Dr. Ken MacFarland of the University of Tennessee, who first introduced me to the fascinating world of succulents. Thanks to Stanley's Greenhouse and the University of Tennessee Gardens, both located in Knoxville, Tennessee, for generously making their plant collections available to photograph.

Thank you to my husband, Jerry Yarnell, for persevering through boring photo sessions. His hands appear in several of the photos.

Aurora Bell, my editor at The Countryman Press, did a wonderful job of keeping me on track and providing constructive suggestions.

A warm note of thanks to my agent, Grace Freedson. We have been working together now for well over a decade.

These are some popular sources for succulents, cacti, and supplies. You can also find sources for a particular plant online.

Plants

Succulent plants can be ordered online from Amazon, Home Depot, and other large retailers. For the hobbyist interested in the less common varieties, several mail-order sources specialize in succulents.

Mountain Crest Gardens:
  mountaincrestgardens.com
Simply Succulents: simplysucculents.com
The Succulent Source: thesucculentsource.com
Leaf and Clay: leafandclay.co
Planet Desert: planetdesert.com

Supplies

Miracle-Gro potting mix and soluble fertilizer are available nationwide.

Greenhouse Megastore:
  www.greenhousemegastore.com
Grower's Solution: www.growerssolution.com
Nursery Supplies, Inc.: www.nurserysupplies.com

Page 6: © kynny/iStockPhoto.com; page 8: © coldsnowstorm/iStockPhoto.com; page 12, 142: © Sara Edwards/iStockPhoto.com; page 15 (top left): © Dugwy/iStockPhoto.com; page 15 (bottom right): © ePhotocorp/iStockPhoto.com; page 16 (top right): © Lcc54613/iStockPhoto .com; page 19 (right): © nikkytok/iStockPhoto .com; page 20: © x-posure/iStockPhoto.com; page 22: © Lya_Cattel/iStockPhoto.com; page 27: © SlobodanMiljevic/iStockPhoto.com; page 35: © KatarzynaBialasiewicz/iStockPhoto.com; page 37 (center): © AnthonyRosenberg/iStockPhoto.com; page 37 (top left): © Kanawa_Studio/iStockPhoto .com; page 37 (top right): © mkos83/iStockPhoto .com; page 37 (bottom left): © Oleksandr Sokurenko/iStockPhoto.com; page 37 (bottom right): © zoomstudio/iStockPhoto.com; page 43: © Neustockimages/iStockPhoto.com; page 48: © imv/iStockPhoto.com; page 50: © jeffadl/ iStockPhoto.com; page 57: © shakzu/iStockPhoto .com; page 60–61: © Africadventures/iStockPhoto .com; page 67: © TanawatPontchour/iStockPhoto .com; page 70: © aerogondo/iStockPhoto.com; page 72: © JillianCain/iStockPhoto.com; page 75: © AndreaObzerova/iStockPhoto.com; page 79: © Alberto Masnovo/iStockPhoto.com; page 83: © SumikoPhoto/iStockPhoto.com; page 85: © skodonnell/iStockPhoto.com; page 94–95: © Greentellect_Studio/iStockPhoto.com; page 96: © mzajac/iStockPhoto.com; page 100: © kitzcorner/ iStockPhoto.com; page 103 (top right): © SzB/ iStockPhoto.com; page 104 (bottom right): © undefined undefined/iStockPhoto.com; page 107: © HaiMinhDuong/iStockPhoto.com; page 116 (top left): © yellowpaul/iStockPhoto.com; page 116 (bottom right): © Exsodus/iStockPhoto.com; page 116 (bottom left): © Jeanine/iStockPhoto.com; page 123 (bottom right): © Andrew Waugh/iStockPhoto.com; page 124, 126: © shihina/iStockPhoto.com; page 129 (top left): © skymoon13/iStockPhoto.com; page 133: © Aneese/iStockPhoto.com; page 137 (top): © krisblackphotography/iStockPhoto.com; page 137 (bottom): © Firn/iStockPhoto.com; page 139 (top right): © Sara Friesz/iStockPhoto.com; page 139 (bottom left): © JordiRoy/iStockPhoto.com; page 140: © Clement Peiffer/iStockPhoto.com; page 144: © THEGIFT777/iStockPhoto.com; page 145: © GaryAlvis/iStockPhoto.com; page 146 (top right): © glennimage/iStockPhoto.com; page 146 (bottom left): © jessicahyde/iStockPhoto.com; page 147: © Elixirpix/iStockPhoto.com; page 151 (top right): © wizdaz/iStockPhoto.com

Note: Page references in *italics* indicate photographs.